MICHIGAN MODERN

AN ARCHITECTURAL LEGACY

BRIAN D. CONWAY

JAMES HAEFNER

McGregor Memorial Conference Center, Wayne State University, Detroit, designed by Minoru Yamasaki (1958).

VISUAL PROFILE BOOKS, INC., NEW YORK

This publication was produced with generous support from:
    General Motors Foundation
    Historic Ford Estates
    Furthermore: a program of the J. M. Kaplan Fund
    Michigan History Foundation
    Michigan State Housing Development Authority
    Michigan Historic Preservation Network

Published by:
Visual Profile Books, Inc.
389 Fifth Avenue, New York, NY 10016
Phone: 212.279.7000
www.visualprofilebooks.com

Distributed by:
National Book Network, Inc.
15200 NBN Way, Blue Ridge Summit, PA 17214
Toll Free (U.S.): 800.462.6420
Toll Free Fax (U.S.): 800.338.4550
Email orders or Inquires: customercare@nbnbooks.com

ISBN 13 : 978-0-9975489-7-6
ISBN 10 : 0-9975489-7-5

Book Designer: Scott Markel
All Photographs: James Haefner, Photographer,
Courtesy Michigan State Historic Preservation Office

*Cranbrook Art Museum and
Library in Bloomfield Hills
designed by Eliel Saarinen (1942).*

3

CONTENTS

7 PREFACE

8 ACKNOWLEDGEMENTS

10 INTRODUCTION

14 ESSAY BY ALAN HESS

18 CRANBROOK EDUCATIONAL COMMUNITY
Eliel Saarinen, 1928-42

34 EDSEL AND ELEANOR FORD HOUSE-GAME ROOM AND BOYS' ROOMS
Walter Dorwin Teague, 1935

40 CHARLES AND INGRID KOEBEL HOUSE
Eliel and Eero Saarinen, 1939-40

48 GREGOR AND ELIZABETH AFFLECK HOUSE
Frank Lloyd Wright, 1941

54 MELVYN MAXWELL AND SARA SMITH HOUSE
Frank Lloyd Wright, 1949-50

60 LOUIS AND JOSEPHINE ASHMUN HOUSE
Alden B. Dow, 1951

68 WILLIAM AND MARY PALMER HOUSE
Frank Lloyd Wright, 1950-51

74 JOHN AND KATHLEEN McLUCAS HOUSE
Alexander Girard, 1950

82 RICHARD AND FLORENCE CRANE HOUSE
Robert C. Metcalf, 1954

90 WILLIAM AND ELIZABETH MUSCHENHEIM HOUSE
William Muschenheim, 1954

98 GENERAL MOTORS TECHNICAL CENTER
Eero Saarinen, 1949-56

112 DOROTHY TURKEL HOUSE
Frank Lloyd Wright, 1956-57

122 JAMES AND SARAH KIRKPATRICK HOUSE
George Nelson, 1957

130 LAFAYETTE PARK
Ludwig Mies van der Rohe, 1956-63

138 HERMAN MILLER MAIN SITE BUILDING
George Nelson, 1958; A. Quincy Jones, 1970

146 McGREGOR MEMORIAL CONFERENCE CENTER
Minoru Yamasaki, 1958

154 JOHN AND MARGARET RIECKER HOUSE
Alden B. Dow, 1961

162 MICHIGAN CONSOLIDATED GAS COMPANY BUILDING
Minoru Yamasaki, 1962-63

166 CONGREGATION SHAAREY ZEDEK SYNAGOGUE
Percival Goodman, 1962-63

170 ST. FRANCIS DE SALES CHURCH
Marcel Breuer, 1964-66

176 ROBERT AND BARBARA SCHWARTZ HOUSE
Robert E. Schwartz, 1964-66

182 W. HAWKINS FERRY HOUSE
William Kessler, 1964

192 DONALD AND HARRIET FREEMAN HOUSE
Gunnar Birkerts, 1965-66

200 UNITED AUTO WORKERS FAMILY EDUCATION CENTER
Oskar Stonorov, 1967-70

212 CHURCH OF ST. MARY
William Wesley Peters, 1969

218 POWER CENTER FOR THE PERFORMING ARTS
Kevin Roche, 1970-71

224 JAMES AND JEAN DOUGLAS HOUSE
Richard Meier, 1971-73

238 MINORU AND TERUKO YAMASAKI HOUSE
Minoru Yamasaki, 1972

244 SHIRLEY S. OKERSTROM FINE ARTS BUILDING
The Architects Collaborative, 1972

250 ALLEN AND ALENE SMITH LAW LIBRARY ADDITION
Gunnar Birkerts, 1978-81

258 SCOTT DEVON HOUSE
Dirk Lohan, 1992

268 CHAMELEON HOUSE
Anderson Anderson Architecture, 2006

278 LINDA DRESNER HOUSE
Steven Sivak, 2011

286 ELI AND EDYTH BROAD ART MUSEUM
Zaha Hadid, 2012

Devon House in Ada designed by Dirk Lohan (1991-92).

Triton Pool leading to the
peristyle connecting the
Art Museum and Library at
Cranbrook in Bloomfield Hills.

PREFACE

I had the good fortune to meet photographer James Haefner in 2013. Jim was interested in the work that I was doing in the State Historic Preservation Office to study and document the history of Michigan's role in American modernism. He decided to make a cold call to introduce himself to me. At our first meeting, Jim brought along a portfolio of beautiful photographs he had taken of some of Southeast Michigan's iconic historic architecture. I immediately became an admirer of his work, and a friendship and partnership developed from that point forward.

Jim Haefner has been a photographer for more than fifty years, successfully creating professional images for clients during the last thirty-eight of them. Educated at the University of New Mexico and the Rochester Institute of Technology, he apprenticed at commercial photography studios in the Detroit, Michigan area. Starting James Haefner Photography in 1979, he immediately made a difference in the automotive advertising arena and his work has been featured in countless automobile advertisements and product literature. His interest in architecture grew out of selecting buildings as backdrops for auto advertising and creating visual solutions that met his client's needs. Jim diversified his practice around 2000 and applied his talents to the art of architectural photography. His love of good design is evident in both his automotive and architectural photography. Revealing the designer's ideas and intentions is the goal of every image he makes. This book captures Jim's appreciation for design-driven concepts that result in buildings.

As the State Historic Preservation Office (SHPO) planned and mounted an exhibition and conducted a symposium at Cranbrook in 2013 entitled Michigan Modern: Design That Shaped America, Jim produced a poster commemorating the event featuring his photograph of the lobby of the Eero Saarinen designed General Motors Technical Center Styling (Design) Building. That poster was distributed to all the participants at the symposium. When the exhibition moved in 2014 to the Grand Rapids Art Museum and a symposium was conducted at Kendall College of Art and Design, the poster was again distributed to participants. Jim's photograph used in that poster has become the symbol for the State Historic Preservation Office's Michigan Modern project and that same photograph was featured on the cover of the SHPO's acclaimed book Michigan Modern: Design That Shaped America that was published in the fall of 2016. That book also incorporated a number of photographs by Jim Haefner.

While I was working on the production of that first book, Jim brought up the idea of doing a collaborative book of photography of Michigan's modern architecture. Knowing the quality of Jim's photography, I jumped at the idea and the chance to work with him. In partnership with the Michigan History Foundation, Jim and I were able to secure funding from the General Motors Foundation, the Historic Ford Estates, the J. M. Kaplan Fund, and the Michigan Historic Preservation Network to make this book a reality.

I had the pleasure and honor of accompanying Jim on several of his photo shoots for the book. I saw the artist in action framing the perfect shot, calling out the details, and waiting for the right lighting. Together with his assistant, he would often be at a site for hours, even days, to get the right shot, all the while making the property owners comfortable with his professional and friendly manner.

Obtaining the collection of photographs for this book has been a wonderful and memorable experience. Friendships developed along the way. Homeowners and business contacts graciously allowed us into their homes and properties. Highlights include soaring in a helicopter over Lake Michigan to get several aerial photographs of Richard Meier's Douglas House, followed by pizza on the rooftop deck at sunset with owners Mike and Marcia; experiencing the detail and changing reflection of light at the Chameleon House near Northport; and watching Jim fly his drone over the Black Lake Conference Center to capture the setting and environment of that complex. I witnessed Jim remove signs, utilize lifts and ladders, and move furniture, but every time putting everything back just as he found it. I learned a lot about architectural photography and have great respect for all that is involved in creating beautiful images.

I had a good sense of Michigan's breadth of architecture after thirty-seven years in the State Historic Preservation Office, as staff architect and then as director, coupled with extensive study and research of modern architecture through the SHPO's Michigan Modern Project. Nevertheless, selecting properties for inclusion in this book was a challenge. The original list had to be narrowed down for manageability, and some buildings had to be eliminated because of their condition, maintenance issues, or owners not wanting to be included in the book. I felt it was important to portray the range of modern architecture from the early works of Eliel Saarinen and Walter Dorwin Teague to more recent outstanding work of Steven Sivak and Zaha Hadid. I also thought it was important to include unique works of lesser-known architects such as Robert E. Schwartz and Anderson Anderson Architects as well as those of well-known architects such as Frank Lloyd Wright and Mies van der Rohe. I listed the architects that are most often attributed to the design of a building, though in most all cases it is a team of architects, engineers, specialists, and contractors that together make the building a reality. In total, the portfolio of diverse architectural work photographed over two summers and portrayed in the book is quite remarkable.

I am honored and privileged to have experienced some of Michigan's greatest modern architecture, all the while developing lasting friendships throughout the production of this book.

Brian D. Conway

ACKNOWLEDGEMENTS

This book production has been a partnership between myself and photographer James Haefner. The book would not be possible without Jim's beautiful photographs. His eye, talent, and technical skill for architectural photography is unsurpassed. Jim's assistant's, Karl Moses and David Dalton, were invaluable in the photography process. Jim has gained my respect and admiration, and I feel privileged to have worked with him on this project.

Of course, the photography would not have been possible without the trust and openness of the property owners and contacts who allowed us to photograph their buildings. Their hospitality, enthusiasm, and general interest in the project was genuine and reaffirming. I made a few new friends along the way and certainly got to experience some remarkable architecture.

The beautiful design of the book is a result of the fine work of Scott Markel, who worked closely with Jim and myself on the final look of the book. I am grateful that Jim made this connection for us, as Jim and Scott worked on several projects together previously.

Thank you to my friend and colleague Alan Hess, architect, architectural historian, and architectural critic, for his insights and contribution with the writing of an essay for the book. I got to know Alan early on in the development of the Michigan Modern Project as he expressed interest and a clear understanding of the importance of Michigan's role in Modernism. He has been a great supporter, advisor, and inspiration for me as my work on Modernism in Michigan has unfolded. He was an important contributor to my first book, Michigan Modern: Design That Shaped America.

I owe a debt of gratitude to my State Historic Preservation Office colleagues Amy Arnold and Todd Walsh for their encouragement, enthusiasm, and assistance in property research and writing for some of the entries in the book. Both Amy and Todd have developed an incredible knowledge of modern architecture and have provided valuable assistance and advice throughout this book project. I also thank colleague Laura Ashlee for her editorial assistance.

A publication of this quality would not be possible without the generous grants and donations made to the Michigan History Foundation to support the production of this book. Generous funding was received from the General Motors Foundation and the Historic Ford Estates, with additional funding from Furthermore: a Program of the J. M. Kaplan Fund, the Michigan Historic Preservation Network, and the Michigan History Foundation.

Brian D. Conway

Main staircase in the Broad Art Museum in East Lansing designed by Zaha Hadid (2012).

INTRODUCTION

Michigan's architecture is broad in style and rich in significance. The state's nineteenth-century architecture ranges from stately Greek Revival houses in Marshall, a "virtual textbook of 19th-century American architecture," to vernacular houses found in the Upper Peninsula's mining company towns, to exuberant Victorian architecture in historic neighborhoods like Heritage Hill in Grand Rapids, to Arts and Crafts Bungalows lining streets in Highland Park, part of Greater Detroit. Michigan's twentieth-century architecture includes masterworks of modern architects such as Eliel Saarinen, Eero Saarinen, Minoru Yamasaki, Frank Lloyd Wright, Ludwig Mies van der Rohe, Marcel Breuer, and Richard Meier. That tradition continues in the twenty-first century with work by Anderson Anderson Architecture, Steven Sivak, and Zaha Hadid. Arranged chronologically, this book's focus on Modern architecture begins with the work of Eliel Saarinen at Cranbrook Educational Community, in Bloomfield Hills, and concludes with Zaha Hadid's acclaimed Eli and Edythe Broad Art Museum, in East Lansing.

This book continues the work of the State Historic Preservation Office in documenting Modernism in Michigan. Known as the Michigan Modern Project, the study started in 2008 with a grant from the Preserve America program of the National Park Service. It combined extensive research and context development with the identification of significant Modern architecture throughout the state. Besides completing a dozen or so listings of Michigan's Modern resources in the National Register of Historic Places, the project saw the elevation of three properties to National Historic Landmark status: General Motors Technical Center, in Warren, designed by Eero Saarinen, Lafayette Park, in Detroit, designed by Mies van der Rohe, and McGregor Memorial Conference Center, in Detroit, designed by Minoru Yamasaki. Eliel Saarinen's Cranbrook campus and the Alden B. Dow Home and Studio had previously been designated as National Historic Landmarks. The project revealed and documented the significant role Michigan played in the development of Modern design, resulting in a major exhibition and symposium held at Cranbrook in 2013. Then, the exhibition traveled to the Grand Rapids Art Museum in 2014, accompanied by a symposium conducted with Kendall College of Art and Design. Michigan Modern culminated in 2016 with the publication of the book Michigan Modern: Design That Shaped America, edited by Amy L. Arnold and myself.

The confluence of industry, education, and architecture in early twentieth-century Michigan put the state at the center of the development of Modernism. Detroit automakers styled the cars that became part of the American Dream; West Michigan furniture companies designed and produced the Modern furniture that transformed America's homes and offices; creative and influential Michigan architects drew talented designers to work in their offices while the state's architecture and design schools were among the first in the nation to teach Modern theory. The interaction between the state's industrial wealth and the public's growing interest in quality architecture was manifested early in the twentieth century in downtown Detroit in buildings such as the dramatic Guardian Building, designed by Wirt Rowland of Smith Hinchman & Grylls, and the lavish Fisher Building, designed by Albert Kahn. This robust economic and cultural foundation led to the strong Modern design ethos that thrives in Michigan today.

The University of Michigan and Cranbrook Academy of Art were early leaders of America's Modern design education. Emil Lorch, the first dean of the University of Michigan's College of Architecture, developed a method of teaching based on the Theory of Pure Design, a theory he mastered during his work at the Chicago Institute of Art and his association with Prairie School architects. This approach–emphasizing originality and geometry without reference to historical styles–was radically different from the Beaux Arts Classicism then being taught at most architecture schools. The list of graduates from Lorch's program is luminous, including Edward Charles Bassett, John E. Dinwiddie, Maynard Lyndon, Charles Willard Moor,

Ralph Rapson, Robert Swanson, and John Dinkeloo. One notable early graduate under Lorch was Joseph Hudnut, who became dean at Harvard Graduate School of Architecture in 1936, and brought Walter Gropius and Marcel Breuer to Harvard. The talented architecture faculty at the University of Michigan branched out with house designs for local clients as Ann Arbor grew. Consequently Ann Arbor, became a living museum of work by Michigan architects such as William Muschenheim and Robert Metcalf as well as prominent visitors like Frank Lloyd Wright.

In 1923, Emil Lorch invited Finnish architect Eliel Saarinen to become a guest instructor at the University of Michigan. A successful architect in his native Finland, Saarinen was acclaimed by American architects for his innovative, second-place-winning design for the Chicago Tribune Tower design competition in 1922. Saarinen had taught for two years at the university when he received an offer from Detroit newspaper publisher George Booth to design a campus for an Arts and Crafts-inspired arts educational community on Booth's estate in Bloomfield Hills, and to assist in developing the institution's curriculum. Booth named both his estate and the school Cranbrook after an ancestral English town.

At Cranbrook, Saarinen created a remarkable campus tracing the evolution of his design philosophy from the 1930s through the 1940s. His conversion to Modernism culminated in the connecting of the Cranbrook Art Museum and Library with the Modern peristyle. Perhaps even more significant is the impact that the curriculum and Cranbrook students had on American modern design. The Arts and Crafts-based holistic approach to teaching design developed such remarkable talents as Eero Saarinen, Charles and Ray Eames, Florence Schust Knoll, Ralph Rapson, Harry Weese, Marianne Strengell, Harry Bertoia, Carl Milles, and Ruth Adler Schnee, to name a few.

As the architectural practices of emerging talented Michigan architects like Eero Saarinen and Minoru Yamasaki grew, they attracted young talent to work in their studios. Many of these recruits, including Gunnar Birkerts, Kevin Roche, William Kessler, Balthazar Korab, John Dinkeloo, and Cesar Pelli, used their experiences to develop notable careers, outstanding portfolios, and names for themselves. While some departed Michigan for far-flung destinations, they took the state's design culture with them.

As Michigan industry flourished in the twentieth century, its impact on American design cannot be overstated. The automotive industry routinely used Modern architecture as backdrop to promote the new automobiles of the future. Automobiles themselves had an unprecedented impact on architecture and city planning. Automobiles became an economic necessity and an aesthetic challenge. Architects responded by turning porte cochères, garages and carports into dominant features in Modern buildings, often to proudly display the latest automobiles. In contrast, Mies designed Lafayette Park, a residential development in Detroit, with depressed parking and landscaping to screen cars from view. Harley Earl, director of design at General Motors, recognized the important connection between autos and architecture by insisting that a well-known architect design the facility where the future of General Motors would be determined. Opening under the tag line of "Where Today Meets Tomorrow," Saarinen's Technical Center became the futuristic backdrop for automobile promotion while setting the standard for modern corporate campus development.

Simultaneously, the West Michigan furniture industry called upon architects to design Modern lines of furniture. Eliel Saarinen, in partnership with his daughter Pipsan Saarinen Swanson and son-in-law J. Robert F. Swanson, designed a furniture line called Flexible Home Arrangement–considered the first commercial introduction of modular furniture–in 1939 for the Johnson Furniture Company in Grand Rapids. D. J. DePree, the head of Herman Miller Furniture Company, hired

Mezzanine level overlooking main lobby of the Fisher Building in Detroit designed by Albert Kahn (1928).

architect George Nelson as the company's second director of design to introduce new Modern furniture. Nelson in turn brought in architect Charles Eames and other Cranbrook graduates to add to the company's furniture lines. Cranbrook alumna Florence Schust Knoll did likewise by hiring fellow Cranbrook graduates to design furniture for Knoll. Because of the furniture industry, Michigan is fortunate to have a number of unique structures designed by these furniture-designing architects, such as the Kirkpatrick House, in Kalamazoo, and the Herman Miller Main Site complex, in Zeeland, both designed by George Nelson; and the Max DePree House, in Zeeland, designed by Charles Eames. Expanding into office furniture, Herman Miller revolutionized office space planning with its development of the Action Office System, heralding the era of open office planning with furniture systems and the ubiquitous cubicals.

Michigan designers and patrons of the arts called upon talented architects to design homes or structures related to the arts. W. Hawkins Ferry, Detroit patron of the arts, hired William Kessler to design a house to display his art collection in Grosse Pointe Shores. Fashion designer Linda Dresner retained Steven Sivak to design her unique house in Birmingham. The Architects Collaborative was commissioned by Northwestern Michigan College to develop and design its Fine

Arts Building in Traverse City. Kevin Roche of Kevin Roche John Dinkeloo Associates, former partner and lead designer in the Eero Saarinen Associates office in Bloomfield Hills, was hired by the University of Michigan to design the Power Center for the Performing Arts. Michigan State University commissioned Zaha Hadid to design the Eli and Edythe Broad Art Museum in East Lansing.

The intertwining of industry, architecture, education and the arts in Michigan is reflected in the structures selected for inclusion in this book. Michigan was at the forefront in the development of Modern design. Its newest architecture celebrates a proud tradition that now extends to the twenty-first century.

Brian D. Conway

Detroit skyline, right to left is the top of the Michigan Consolidated Gas Company Building, Minoru Yamasaki (1962-63); One Detroit Center, John Burgee and Phillip Johnson (1991-93); and Guardian Building (1928-29), Buhl Building (1925), and Penobscott Building (1928), each designed by Wirt Rowland of Smith, Hinchman &Grylls.

Lobby of the Guardian Building in Detroit designed by
Wirt Rowland of Smith, Hinchman & Grylls, (1928-29).

FERTILE GROUND: MICHIGAN'S MODERNIST REVOLUTION

ESSAY BY ALAN HESS

Michigan's role in the architectural revolution that championed Modernism is a true story that must be told. By the end of the nineteenth century the Industrial Revolution had sparked architectural revolutions around the world. History books spotlight Chicago's radically creative skyscrapers in the 1890s, and the Bauhaus' fascination with the machine's possibilities and imagery in 1919. Rarely, however, do these books give equal attention to events in Michigan that helped generate a distinctive Modern architecture in those same years. Some of Michigan's significant Modern buildings—including Albert Kahn's River Rouge plant and Eero Saarinen's General Motors Technical Center—are routinely mentioned, but the story of the broader culture that produced these and other masterpieces is usually neglected.

It isn't simply that Michigan participated in the major trends of global Modernism. The state was an active and decisive player, boasting the third largest collection of Frank Lloyd Wright structures in the United States, and Mies van der Rohe's Lafayette Park housing complex, the largest grouping of his structures anywhere. Walter Dorwin Teague's interiors at Edsel Ford's estate in Grosse Pointe Shores are a pinnacle of Art Moderne design. Michigan has continued to engage in the international conversation with works by such famous architects as Marcel Breuer, The Architects Collaborative, Richard Meier, Dirk Lohan and Zaha Hadid that are shaping today's built environment.

The more significant story, however, is how Michigan developed a Modern sensibility largely from its own grass roots, grown from seeds no one had to import from abroad. Because of the auto industry, the state had a visceral understanding of modern mass production and mass marketing for the public. It was turning new technology—the mother's milk of Modernism—into a new way of life that stretched across society from the executive suites of the car industry to the workers on the assembly lines. Michigan democratized Modernism.

This innovative culture produced a diversity of ideas ranging from Alden Dow's warm and expressive organic designs to Mies's minimalist glass boxes. It launched the exploration of a spectrum of building types, from factories and vacation homes to office parks and shopping centers. The fruits of its experimentation fed the growing needs of suburbia.

Michigan's innovations in suburban residential design by William Muschenheim, Robert Metcalf, Alden Dow, Robert Schwartz, William Kessler, Alexander Girard, George Nelson, and others have largely escaped recognition as a collective phenomenon. Yet they deserve no less attention than the Case Study Program in California, the work of O'Neill Ford, Mackie and Kamrath, and Donald Barthelme in Texas, the accomplishments of George Fred Keck, Harry Weese, and Bertrand Goldberg in Chicago, and the Sarasota School in Florida. None of these groupings arose randomly. They arose from specific cultural, educational, and economic conditions of locale, just as their counterparts in Michigan did.

THE CAR DRIVES THE MICHIGAN REVOLUTION

The best efforts in Michigan embodied a distinct approach to Modern design. Its ethos would spread worldwide, beginning with Albert Kahn and Eliel Saarinen. Michigan's industry and culture shaped their creative talents in ways no other region would duplicate.

Harley Earls' 1938 Buick Y-Job concept car in the Eero Saarinen-designed General Motors Styling Auditorium.

As early as 1903, Albert Kahn's factory buildings for Packard, Ford, Dodge, and other automakers became landmarks of pure Modern design. Direct expressions of their functional purpose, they utilized technologically advanced concrete and glass to create large, efficient open spaces. They paid no homage to traditional taste or style. What Chicago had done for the office skyscraper a decade earlier, Kahn did for the factory, revolutionizing the industry at the heart of the American economy.

The buildings that produced the cars were designed with as much practicality, simplification, and strength as the carburetors, axles, and chassis of the cars themselves. Kahn himself would spread this radical conception around the world, all the way to the Soviet Union, but he would also influence many later stellar factory designs by Alvar Aalto, Brinkman and Van der Vlugt, and even the Futurist fantasies of Antonio Sant'Elia. Kahn's influence on the next generation of European Modernists—Mies van der Rohe, Walter Gropius, and Le Corbusier—confirms his seminal role in global Modernism.

In fact, Kahn's pragmatic technological innovations have continued to influence Michigan Modernism and generate the exciting atmosphere that attracts ambitious young architects to the state. The technical refinement of concrete that started with Kahn and his brother Julius has advanced in Michigan with the work of Kevin Roche and John Dinkeloo at the University of Michigan's Power Center for the Performing Arts, Gunnar Birkerts's University of Michigan Law Library, Marcel Breuer's beton brut St. Frances de Sales Church, Percival Goodman's Shaarey Zedek Synagogue, Alden Dow's Unit Block Houses, and more recently Steven Sivak's Dresner House. The transformation of the heroic heavy industry factories of the early twentieth century economy by Kahn evolved during midcentury into Herman Miller's Zeeland campus, originally designed by George Nelson and subsequently expanded by A. Quincy Jones, where a lighter fabrication system and a new concern for the workers' environment are seen.

A FINNISH VISIONARY ARRIVES

Eliel Saarinen's reputation was already established when he arrived in Chicago from Finland in the early 1920s. Accepting George Booth's offer to create a school based on Arts and Crafts principles in Bloomfield Hills, Michigan, Saarinen began the development of the Cranbrook Educational Community with a master plan and designs for its first structures. Over the next quarter century the buildings traced the evolution of his vision. His first buildings for the Cranbrook School for Boys (1928) echo his work in Finland. But he quickly moved on to Kingswood School for Girls (1931) as a clean, broad-eaved expression of the horizontal lines of American Modernism, enriched by brickwork, furniture, tapestries, and other crafted details integrated into the architecture. It dovetailed with the color, rich detail, and opulence seen in the Chicago School, the Prairie School, and Organic architecture, well represented in Michigan by Frank Lloyd Wright, Alden Dow, and William Wesley Peters.

Pushing his ideas further, Saarinen took the Cranbrook Institute of Science (1937) and Art Museum and Library (1942) into new territory, where simplification did not sacrifice richness of ornament, proportions, or integration with landscaped settings. Saarinen thus defined Michigan Modernism as a synthesis of his earlier Arts and Crafts principles, taking fresh forms that expressed modern life with an appreciation for the detail and care of handcraft, and combining them with Detroit's devotion to modern mass production. The compatibility of the two concepts was not obvious, yet they jointly offered a distinct alternative to the mechanistic absolutes of the International Style. Saarinen's ideas applied equally well at the residential scale in the Koebel House (1939.) In contrast to the lightweight steel and glass pavilions that Richard Neutra was designing in Los Angeles at the same time, or the elegant International Style compositions of Edward Durell Stone's Goodyear House, the Koebel House exemplified a distinct Modernism expressive of the Michigan milieu.

Not surprisingly, Eliel's son Eero contributed to the later Cranbrook buildings and the Koebel House. His own revolutionary buildings would spring from this apprenticeship. Underlying the work of both Saarinens was the creative tension between pragmatic modern means and crafted form. Born in Finland, Eero grew up in Michigan and worked alongside his father, mother Loja, and sister Pipsan at Cranbrook from a young age. Largely unconcerned with the strict guidelines of the International Style, he would explore curvilinear forms, irregular geometries, mass produced automotive technology—all Modern, but with an open, exploratory attitude, an interest in richness, and a popular appeal that could be seen also in the work of Minoru Yamasaki, William Kessler, Alden Dow—and not coincidentally in the auto stylists at GM, Ford and Chrysler. This more expressionistic and less doctrinaire outlook distinguished Michigan's Modernism.

The timing was right for change. Although the International Style was ascendant in the profession at midcentury, its continued vitality was being questioned in many quarters. Michigan offered another path to Modernism, and Eero Saarinen followed it in his first major commission, the General Motors Technical Center, in Warren. Drawing on the technical expertise and democratizing reach of the auto industry, Eero Saarinen partnered with Harley Earl, head of GM's Styling Section, to define a new building type for the nation's emerging suburbs: the research office park.

ARCHITECTURE FOR THE SUPERHIGHWAY

The GM Tech Center has long been interpreted as Saarinen's version of the Miesian International Style. Certainly there are similarities between GM Tech and Mies's Illinois Institute of Technology, with its balanced abstract arrangement of clean geometric structures of steel, glass and brick. This interpretation, however, overlooks all the significant nuances of this design by a Michigan architect for the ultimate Michigan client. Saarinen and Earl had something very different in mind than an International Style campus. Their project had to embody the full power and glory of General Motor's technical prowess and economic hegemony as the largest corporation in the free world, and the International Style was not up to the task.

So Saarinen and his team drew directly from the technological innovations of the auto industry. Curtain walls frame their glass in neoprene gaskets taken directly from windshield technology. Brilliantly colored ceramic brick surfaces (a decidedly non-Miesian feature) were developed with the technical know-how of GM's spark plug division and the ceramic artists of Cranbrook—with a nod to the rainbow of paint colors available in GM's cars. Detail after detail, from integrated sprinkler/lighting/ventilating ceilings to suspended stairs, transcend Miesian austerity in favor of the aesthetic exuberance reflected in popular automobiles. The Center's campus raceway around a central artificial lake eschews the aloof Cartesian grid of IIT for the superhighway of the American future, cruised by Harley Earl's dream cars and ringed with idealized American roadside architecture. Instead of relying on quiet abstraction, it is punctuated by vivid shapes: the tri-legged stainless steel water tower rising from the lake, the low dome of the Styling Auditorium, and the diaphanous curtain of Alexander Calder's water wall.

Nevertheless, the significance of Michigan Modern was missed by most critics at the time. The partnership of Eero Saarinen, respected but creatively unpredictable, and Harley Earl, chastised by high art critics for the "excesses" of tailfins and chrome, is one of the high points of Modern architecture. Blending advanced technology and the creative talents of architects and engineers, the Center definitively summarizes Michigan's homegrown Modernism, making Modern architecture understandable and acceptable to the wider public.

GM Tech is but one example. Alden Dow's buildings often drew directly from the laboratories of Dow Chemical. Robert Schwartz's dome-capped Robert and Barbara Schwartz House, in Midland, is an elegant prototype for a rapidly constructed polystyrene construction system. And Minoru Yamasaki helped to bring a new dimension to Modern architecture with Neo-Formalism.

Though favoring the International Style early in his career, Yamasaki was transformed in the mid 1950s while on a world tour prompted by his health. Experiencing global architecture and history in-person for the first time, he began working out an original concept, modern in its use of structures and materials, but freed from theories that stripped architecture of its contextual heritage. A striking example of how Yamasaki reintroduced ornament, varied geometries, historical references, serenity, and humanism is his design for McGregor Memorial Conference Center at Wayne State University. This sparkling and weightless building, where the structural columns and capitals meld into a crystalline, light-filled central space filled with movement and energy, sits in pools of water that set off its classical symmetry. Blending ornament and structure, playing with light, evoking the history of architecture in its white marble walls, McGregor Center lays the groundwork for what would later be labeled Postmodernism. Yamasaki, like Edward Durell Stone, William Pereira, John Carl Warnecke, and other Neo-Formalist architects, saved Modernism from a dead end.

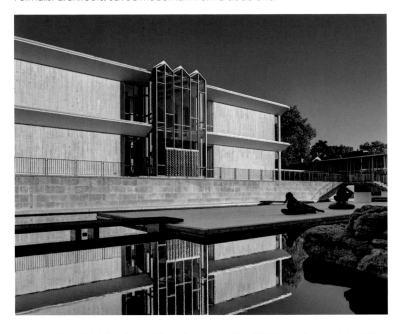

Yamasaki would take these ideas further at the Michigan Consolidated Gas Building, a skyscraper anchoring the foot of Detroit's Woodward Boulevard, the city's main arterial. In place of the static grid of International Style high rises, Yamasaki emphasizes the verticality implicit in the tall office building artistically considered. The tri-partite composition of Louis Sullivan's skyscrapers is reflected here in a jewel-like lobby of glass and marble set in intricate geometries, a central shaft clad in tall, slender window frames, and a penthouse diadem topped with a blue gas flame. Instead of a dematerialized curtainwall, the facade is reified with deeply faceted precast concrete panels. Rich in ornament, incorporating imagery beyond the mechanistic, the Michigan Consolidated Gas tower also saluted Detroit's skyscraper tradition of the 1920s, highlighted by Wirt Rowland's colorful Guardian Building and cliff-like gray limestone Penobscot Building, and Albert Kahn's Fisher Building, with its stepped-back upper stories. These buildings were the equal of contemporary Art Deco skyscrapers in New York, Chicago and Los Angeles.

RECOVERING MICHIGAN'S ROLE IN MODERNISM

Why, then, has Michigan's central role in the history of Modernism not been fully recognized? The reasons are numerous and not necessarily related. For example, Albert Kahn has not been fully embraced as a Modernist because many of his residential and public designs were traditional in style, rendering him an imperfect model in historians' eyes. Eero Saarinen has certainly been recognized as a major Modernist, but because so many of his landmarks are national—Dulles International Airport, TWA Flight Center, Gateway Arch and so on—he is not often acknowledged as a Michigan architect in the way that a gifted individual like Richard Neutra is recognized as a Los Angeles architect.

Then there is the case of Minoru Yamasaki, the other major Michigan practitioner who won national acclaim in midcentury. Though he was recognized by both professional and general audiences, his reputation came under attack in a broad critical backlash against Neo-Formalism in the mid-1960s that considered the style too "impure" in comparison to the International Style that dominated Modernism. Yamasaki and fellow Neo-Formalists were dismissed as mere ornamentalists, cluttering clean Modern forms with unnecessary decoration. Art critics also derided Detroit's auto designs for the same reasons. Without powerful Michigan-based critics, journals, museums, or academies to articulate and defend its roots and theories, Michigan's contributions were downgraded or ignored.

Yet Michigan would nonetheless have a broad impact on the course of Modern architecture. Cranbrook Academy and the offices of Saarinen and Yamasaki produced a host of architects who shaped architecture in the later twentieth century: Kevin Roche, John Dinkeloo, Cesar Pelli, Gunnar Birkerts, Charles Bassett, and Ralph Rapson—though most moved away from Michigan. A strong Modernist axis developed between Detroit and Los Angeles, two creative cities defined by the automobile, as Ray and Charles Eames, Victor Gruen and others blazed new trails in Modern architecture, interior design, furniture, and planning. Yet even when these architects gained fame, the role of Michigan in their development flew under the radar. Such are the vagaries of historiography, which are only now being corrected.

Modernism was never a single seed spreading from Europe out to the world. It was many seeds that sprang up in many places out of highly diverse conditions, all seeking the sun of Modern possibilities. Michigan was fertile ground, with the people, vision, and artifacts to prove it.

Alan Hess, architect and historian, has authored nineteen books on Mid-century Modern architecture and urbanism. They include monographs on architects Oscar Niemeyer, Frank Lloyd Wright, and John Lautner, as well as architectural histories of Las Vegas and Palm Springs. Hess's other books include Googie: Ultramodern Roadside Architecture, Forgotten Modern, and The Ranch House. His next book is a history of California Modern Architecture 1900-1975. Hess was a National Arts Journalism Program Fellow at Columbia University's School of Journalism, and a Graham Foundation grant recipient. Active in the preservation of post-World War II architecture, he has written several National Register of Historic Places nominations for significant Mid-century Modern buildings, including the oldest McDonald's drive-in restaurant, and received awards from the National Trust, DOCOMOMO/US, and the Los Angeles Conservancy.

CRANBROOK EDUCATIONAL COMMUNITY

ELIEL SAARINEN, 1928-42

BLOOMFIELD HILLS.

Cranbrook, often referred to as the cradle of American Modernism, is one of the most important groups of educational and architectural structures in America. Today known as Cranbrook Educational Community, the original campus as designed by Eliel Saarinen consists of Cranbrook School for Boys (1928), the Arts and Crafts Building (Art Academy) (1928-29), Faculty Residences, including the Saarinen House (1928-30), Kingswood School for Girls (1930-31), Cranbrook Institute of Science (1937), and Cranbrook Art Museum and Library (1942). The campus also includes Cranbrook House, designed by Albert Kahn as the home of founders George and Ellen Scripps Booth. In keeping with the history of architectural excellence, the campus has continued to grow with significant newer buildings including the Natatorium, designed by Tod Williams and Billie Tsien (1998-99); the New Studios Building, designed by Rafael Moneo (2001-02); Stephen Holl's addition to Cranbrook Institute of Science (1998); and the Collections Wing and restoration of the Saarinen Art Museum, by SmithGroupJJR (2011). The three hundred-acre campus also contains many significant landscape features such as lakes, fountains, sculpture, bridges, courtyards, gardens, outbuildings, and an outdoor performance theater.

George and Ellen Scripps Booth were visionaries who believed they should build something lasting and valuable with their lives and financial resources. (Booth and his father-in-law, James E. Scripps, founded and built the Detroit News into the Booth News publishing empire.) In 1904 they purchased land north of Detroit in present-day Bloomfield Hills to build a new home and to realize a vision. The Booths commissioned Albert Kahn to design and construct a home on the property. Moving into the Tudor Revival-style house in 1908, they named the estate Cranbrook after a village in England where George's father was born. Yet Booth, a proponent of the Arts and Crafts movement and founder and supporter of the Detroit Society of Arts and Crafts, wanted to play a more active role in the arts. Inspired by the American Academy in Rome, the Booths set out to create a fellowship of students where creativity could thrive, with an art academy at the center of the vision and goal. The boys' and girls' schools were part of the means to accomplish that goal. Talented artists would be identified and chosen from the schools and teamed with promising students from elsewhere in the art academy.

The Booths created the Booth Foundation in 1927 with documents foreseeing an arts and crafts school including departments of architecture, design, interior decoration, drawing, painting, sculpture, drama, landscape design, music, and artistic craftsmanship. That evolved into a concept of four master artists-in-residence: an architect, a painter, a sculptor, and a designer—each residing and working at Cranbrook to provide guidance to students.

The Booths began to realize their vision through the fortuitous connection with Eliel Saarinen, who had a similar vision. Saarinen was a successful Finnish architect who came to America's attention through his second-place-winning design entry in the architectural competition for the construction of the Chicago Tribune Tower in 1922. Shortly thereafter, Emil Lorch, the dean of the University of Michigan's College of Architecture, invited Saarinen to come to the university as a visiting instructor. Booth was introduced to Saarinen through his son Henry, an architecture student at the time. Saarinen shared Booth's interest in a school related to the arts and was commissioned by Booth to join his effort and design the campus. Together they developed the Cranbrook plan, with Saarinen becoming the president of the Art Academy in 1932.

The first complex to be designed and built on campus was Cranbrook School for Boys in 1928, followed by the Arts and Crafts Building in 1928-29. The progression of Saarinen's thinking and design philosophy can be seen in subsequent designs and building construction, culminating with the modern and timeless Art Museum and Library and the simplified, yet elegant and dramatic, peristyle connector. By 1929, Booth suggested a girls' school to be called Kingswood School for Girls. The outcome was a Saarinen family project with Eliel designing the school, his wife Loja designing all the woven fabric and rugs, his son Eero designing the furniture, and his daughter Pipsan decorating the auditorium. Similarly, the Saarinen family home, built in 1928-30 and located among faculty houses at the entrance to the campus, was designed as a family project showing the talents of each family member.

Art was strategically incorporated throughout the grounds. At the approach to the Art Museum and Library is the Orpheus Fountain by Carl Milles, which features eight life-size graceful bronze figures listening to music. Swedish sculptor Milles came to Cranbrook at the invitation of Saarinen in 1931 and by 1940 became director of the Sculpture Department, producing over seventy sculptures installed at Cranbrook.

The academy was not considered an art school in the traditional sense, but rather an environment for students to develop creative work with guidance of masters. Indeed, this proved to be a successful model. Among the talented students and instructors who emerged from the academy in the early years were Charles and Ray Eames, Harry Weese, Harry Bertoia, Florence Schust Knoll, Ben Baldwin, Ralph Rapson, Gyo Obata, Cesar Pelli, Kevin Roche, Carl Fiess, Fumihiko Maki, Edmund Bacon, Ruth Adler Schnee, Marshall Fredericks, Carl Milles, Maija Grotell, Wallace Mitchell, and Marianne Strengell, as well as Eero Saarinen.

Cranbrook was listed in the National Register of Historic Places in March 1973 and was listed as a National Historic Landmark in June 1989.

Living Room in the Saarinen House at Cranbrook, Eliel Saarinen with fabrics by Loja Saarinen.

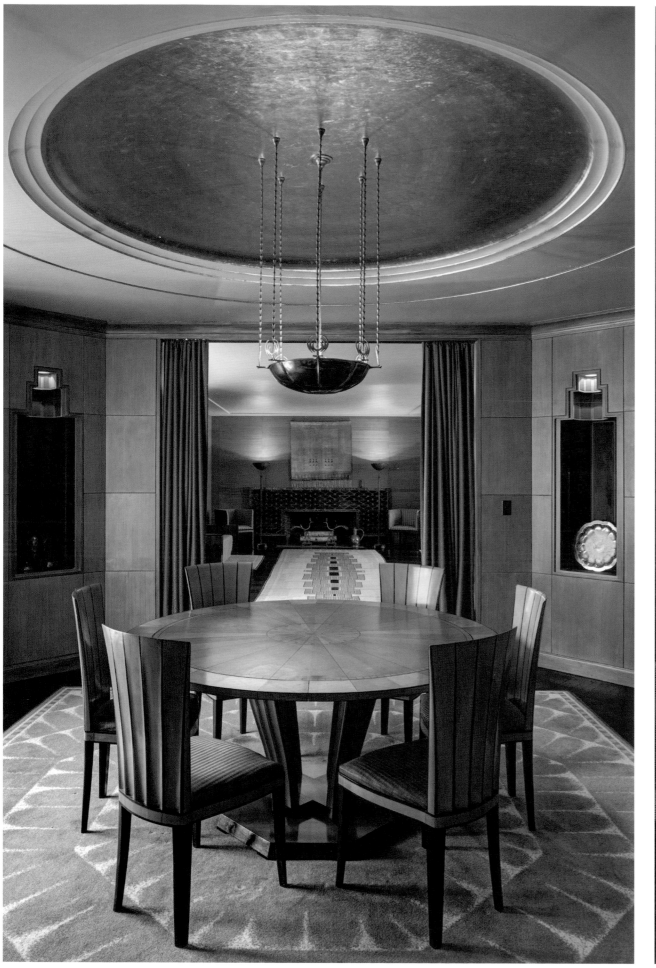

Kingswood School for Girls at Cranbrook, Eliel Saarinen (1931).

Above, Auditorium in Kingswood School for Girls at Cranbrook, Eliel Saarinen (1931).
Right, Dining hall in Kingswood School for Girls at Cranbrook, Eliel Saarinen (1931).

Left, Lobby in Kingswood School for Girls at Cranbrook, Eliel Saarinen (1931).
Above, Main staircase in Kingswood School for Girls at Cranbrook, Eliel Saarinen (1931).

Orpheus Fountain by Carl Milles (1937) in front of the Cranbrook Art Museum.

EDSEL AND ELEANOR
FORD HOUSE
GAME ROOM AND BOYS' ROOMS

WALTER DORWIN TEAGUE, 1935

GROSSE POINTE SHORES.

Edsel Bryant Ford was born in Detroit in 1893 and was the only child of Henry Ford, the founder of the Ford Motor Company, and Clara Jane Bryant Ford. Edsel grew up tinkering with cars alongside his father and was groomed to take over the family business. He married Eleanor Lowthian Clay, and together they had four children. In 1906, Edsel commissioned Albert Kahn to design a family home on land known as Gaukler Point, overlooking Lake St. Clair. Kahn had designed Ford factories utilizing the revolutionary Kahn System of Reinforced Concrete developed by his engineer brother Julius that enabled large open floor plates for the automobile manufacturing production line. Kahn's factory designs were admired worldwide and became an inspiration for modern architectural design. However, the design Kahn created for Ford and his family did not reflect a Modernist style. Collaborating with landscape architect Jens Jensen, Kahn designed a residential complex for the Fords reminiscent of Cotswold villages they had admired in England. The Fords were important patrons of the arts in Detroit, and their selection of Kahn, Jensen, and later Walter Dorwin Teague to create their estate is testament to their love of good design.

Edsel's enthusiasm for aesthetics led him to introduce a sense of design into the Ford Motor Company product lineup in the 1920s. With the help of designer Jozef Galamb, Edsel designed the body of the Ford Model A, a huge step forward from the boxy Model T to which Henry Ford had been so loyal. The Ford Model A , first produced in 1927, was a huge success for the company. From then on, Edsel worked closely with Ford's chief designer Bob Gregorie in shaping the look of Ford automobiles. He was largely responsible for the streamlined 1936 Lincoln Zephyr and the luxurious 1939 Lincoln Continental, both milestones in automobile design.

Throughout the 1930s Edsel raised the level of design for Ford Motor Company's pavilions and new-product exhibits at world's fairs, auto shows, and dealer showrooms by retaining architect and industrial designer Walter Dorwin Teague. Among Teague's major designs for Ford were the Ford pavilions at the 1933 Century of Progress Exposition in Chicago, the 1935 California Pacific International Exposition in San Diego, and the 1939-40 New York World's Fair. Teague, a prolific designer who is considered one of the founding fathers of industrial design along with Raymond Loewy and Henry Dreyfuss, was a shrewd choice for Ford. In 1944, he joined forces with Loewy and Dreyfuss to establish the Society of Industrial Design (SID) and served as its first president. (SID evolved into the Industrial Design Society of America in 1965.)

Edsel engaged Teague in the mid-1930s to redesign several rooms in the family home. The streamlined and modern rooms Teague designed contrast with the traditional Tudor Revival-style rooms elsewhere in the Albert Kahn-designed house. Teague's renovations, a game room on the main floor and boys' bedrooms and sitting room on the second floor, were intended for use by the Fords' teenage children. They are dramatically modern with sleek, custom-made furnishings of exotic hardwoods, recessed lighting reflected in mirrored surfaces, leather-paneled walls, and such signature Teague motifs as streamlined seating, built-in radios, plastic-topped tables, and industrial metallic finishes in copper and brass.

The Edsel and Eleanor Ford House was listed in the National Register of Historic Places in July 1979, and listed as a National Historic Landmark in November 2016.

Boys' sitting room.

Left, Game room, Right, Cabinet in game room.

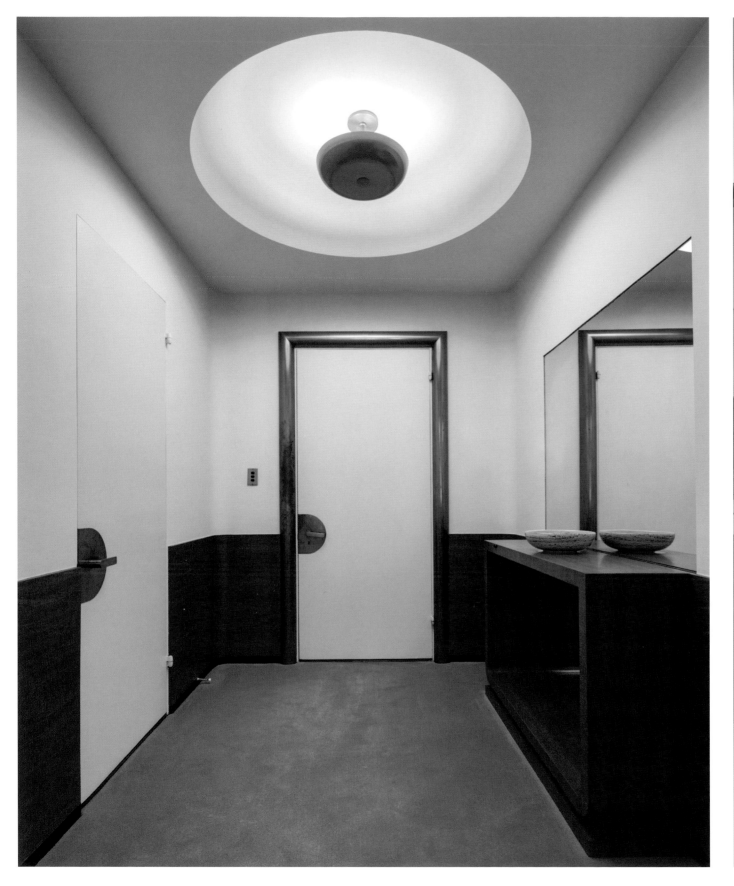

Left, Entrance hallway to boys' sitting room and bedroom.
Above, Boys' bedroom.

CHARLES AND INGRID
KOEBEL HOUSE

ELIEL AND EERO SAARINEN, 1939-40

GROSSE POINTE FARMS.

The father and son team of Eliel and Eero Saarinen designed the Koebel House for Charles and Ingrid Koebel in 1937. The Koebels had met Eliel and Loja Saarinen on board a ship sailing from Scandinavia to the United States some years earlier. Charles Koebel, owner of the Koebel Diamond Tool Company in Detroit, which produced cutting tools for Detroit automakers incorporating industrial diamonds, recalled that personal connection to turn to Saarinen when it came time to build a house.

The design became a Saarinen family project. Eliel's daughter Pipsan Saarinen Swanson and son-in-law J. Robert F. Swanson were responsible for the interior design. Textiles and rugs for the house were designed by Loja Saarinen, Eliel's wife, and executed in her studio at Cranbrook. Lillian Swann Saarinen, Eero's wife at the time, created three sculptures for the dining room niches. Swanson prepared the final working drawings, making a few alterations while keeping the basic design as originally conceived by the Saarinens. It would add another illustrious chapter to the Saarinen success story in America.

Gottlieb Eliel Saarinen was born in 1873 and had a successful career as an architect in his native Finland before launching a successful second career in the United States. He moved his family to America in 1923 after winning the second-place prize in the Chicago Tribune Tower design competition for a stepped back design that strongly influenced the development of the modern skyscraper. Saarinen was initially invited to Michigan to serve as a visiting instructor at the University of Michigan's College of Architecture by dean Emil Lorch. In 1924, George C. Booth, a wealthy newspaper publisher, asked Saarinen to become the chief architect of a new art academy Booth planned to establish in Bloomfield Hills, Michigan. Booth envisioned an international school of art and design incorporating traditions of the Arts and Crafts movement, and Saarinen created the campus master plan and designed many of the buildings on the 178-acre campus. Working together, the two men also developed the curriculum for Cranbrook Academy of Art, combining elements of the Arts and Crafts philosophy with the Bauhaus idea of total design. Cranbrook would become one of the most respected design education centers in America. Saarinen's own family house on the campus, designed as a Saarinen family project and completed in 1930, has many elements that are echoed in the Koebel house.

Eero Saarinen studied sculpture at the Academie de la Grand Chaumiere in Paris before studying architecture at Yale University. He returned to Cranbrook in 1936 to teach and practice architecture in partnership with his father, forming Saarinen and Saarinen in 1937. Father and son, sometimes with J. Robert F. Swanson, collaborated on many projects in the late 1930s and early 1940s, including Crow Island School in Winnetka, Illinois; the Tabernacle Church of Christ in Columbus, Indiana; and the Kleinhans Music Hall in Buffalo, New York. They also received first place in an influential design competition for the Smithsonian Art Gallery in 1939 (unbuilt). After his father's death in 1950, Saarinen went on to be recognized as one of the most important American architects of the twentieth century with his designs for the General Motors Technical Center in Warren, Michigan; the TWA Terminal at Idlewild (John F. Kennedy) Airport in New York; Dulles International Airport outside Washington D.C.; and the monumental Gateway Arch at the Jefferson Expansion Memorial in St. Louis, Missouri. He also made lasting achievements in furniture design. Early in his career while an instructor at Cranbrook, Saarinen worked with Charles Eames in designing formed or molded plywood furniture, including two pieces that won first prizes in the Organic Design Competition sponsored by the Museum of Modern Art in New York in 1940. His pedestal "tulip" table and chairs and his "womb chair" are icons produced by the Knoll Furniture Company, whose former president, Michigan native Florence Schust Knoll, attended Cranbrook's Kingswood School for Girls and became very close to the Saarinen family.

This would not be the Saarinen family's only foray into furniture design. Around the time the house was being built Eliel Saarinen, together with Pipsan and J. Robert Swanson, developed a concept for a line of modern furniture that could be used in varying combinations to meet individual space needs. Partly on the strength of furniture designed for the Koebel House, they developed prototypes for flexible and functional furniture. The Johnson Furniture Company of Grand Rapids, Michigan, began production of Saarinen-Swanson Flexible Home Arrangements, known as FHA, one of the first lines of modular furniture designed for interchangeability and grouping.

The Charles and Ingrid Koebel House was listed in the National Register of Historic Places in December 2009.

Sitting nook off living room.

Dining area with nooks displaying sculpture by Lillian Swann Saarinen.

GREGOR AND ELIZABETH AFFLECK HOUSE

FRANK LLOYD WRIGHT, 1941

BLOOMFIELD HILLS.

The Affleck House is a dramatic, raised Usonian house of brick and cypress designed by Frank Lloyd Wright. Wright designed seventy homes for Michigan clients with over thirty actually built, most from his Usonian and late periods. The Affleck House stands out due to its cantilevered living area and deck that reach out over a wooded ravine. It nestles along a gentle grade before the living area stretches out over a small stream bed toward a ravine and pond. The stream, though now dry, ran under the raised portion of the house. At the center of the house, a massive vertical brick shaft containing the fireplace, kitchen, and utilities anchors the house to the site and counterbalances the broad horizontal cantilevered carport leading to the entry.

Wright first developed his concept for a small, low-cost, well-designed and pleasant house for the modern American family in the 1930s, calling it the Usonian house, while developing his vision for communities. A typical Usonian house is affordable, compact yet functional in its design, and built on a concrete pad, eliminating the basement and the attic space to make it more cost effective. Its plans revolve around a central core including a massive fireplace, kitchen and utility core. The open living and dining area provide the major focus opening to the exterior, with small bedrooms typically lined up along a hall or gallery approached off the central entry. Carports are integral to the design, acknowledging the automobile's importance in the American way of life.

Wright designed Usonian homes in five basic floor plan shapes: polliwog, diagonal, in-line, hexagonal, and raised. The Affleck House combines Wright's in-line and raised Usonian plans, and is planned on a four-by-four-foot grid with tinted red concrete floors. Its central entry loggia explodes from the low-ceilinged entry to a one-and-one-half story height as it flows into the living area. The loggia is bright with skylights above and an interior light-well overlooking the stream bed below, which serves to bring cool air up into the house. A half level up from the loggia, the bedroom hallway or gallery leads to three bedrooms.

The living-dining-kitchen area revolves around the massive central fireplace. The sweeping, forty-four-foot cantilevered living area opens onto a balcony across the full width and wraps around the corner. Its built-in furniture and finely crafted interior woodwork and open ceilings, so characteristic of Wright's work, is a testament to the craftsmanship of Harold Turner, the builder responsible for the construction of almost all of Wright's Michigan homes of this period. (Turner also designed and built several homes in Michigan on his own while following Wright's principles.)

Gregor and Elizabeth Affleck commissioned Wright to design their home in 1940. Mr. Affleck, a Chicago-born chemical engineer, became familiar with Wright's architecture as a youth growing up near Spring Green, Wisconsin. TThe memory of those buildings stayed with him long after graduating from the University of Wisconsin in 1919, and becoming the successful inventor of a fast-drying durable paint that that is still used by Detroit's automotive industry today. When the Afflecks asked Wright to design their house, he instructed them to find a parcel of land outside the city that seemed unbuildable and undesirable. The Afflecks chose a parcel of land that had been subdivided for development but remained unsold due to the topography. The site, which was at the time isolated, densely wooded with no level ground, and bisected by a stream leading to a pond, allowed Wright to explore and further develop his "home for sloping ground," first introduced as part of his Broadacre City concept. A model of the Affleck House was included in the exhibit, Frank Lloyd Wright, American Architect, shown at New York City's Museum of Modern Art, in 1940.

The Affleck House could easily have taken its place in Broadacre City. As early as the 1920s, Wright felt cities were becoming uninhabitable and began exploring ideas to create better living environments. His practice was cut short by the Great Depression, but this gave him time to establish the Taliesin Fellowship in 1932 and experiment with a philosophy for urban planning he termed Broadacre City. The Taliesin Fellowship completed a twelve-by-twelve-foot model of Broadacre City that was displayed at the Industrial Arts Exposition at Rockefeller Center in New York City in 1935 before traveling to several cities across the country. The model illustrated Wright's integration of urban, rural, and suburban communities as well his social and economic views. With Broadacre City as his philosophical base, Wright entered into his second great phase of residential design with his Usonian house.

Though no Broadacre City-type Usonian community was ever completed, two cooperative ventures established by employees of the Upjohn Company, a pharmaceutical manufacturer in Kalamazoo, Michigan, were started based on Broadacre City concepts with Wright designing the homes to be built by the homeowners themselves. Because the group split–some wanted to be in the city of Kalamazoo while others preferred a more rural setting–two partially completed Usonian communities emerged in Michigan, Parkwyn Village in Kalamazoo and The Acres in rural Galesburg. (The Acres is listed in the National Register of Historic Places.)

The Affleck House was built in 1941 before residential construction halted during World War II. The Afflecks were more than satisfied clients, and commissioned Wright a decade later to design a second home for their adjoining lot. "Pergola House," designed in 1952, was never built even though full working drawings were competed. In 1972, the Affleck's two children donated their family house to the College of Architecture and Design at Lawrence Institute of Technology, now Lawrence Technological University, in Southfield, Michigan.

The Gregor and Elizabeth Affleck House was listed in the National Register of Historic Places in October 1998.

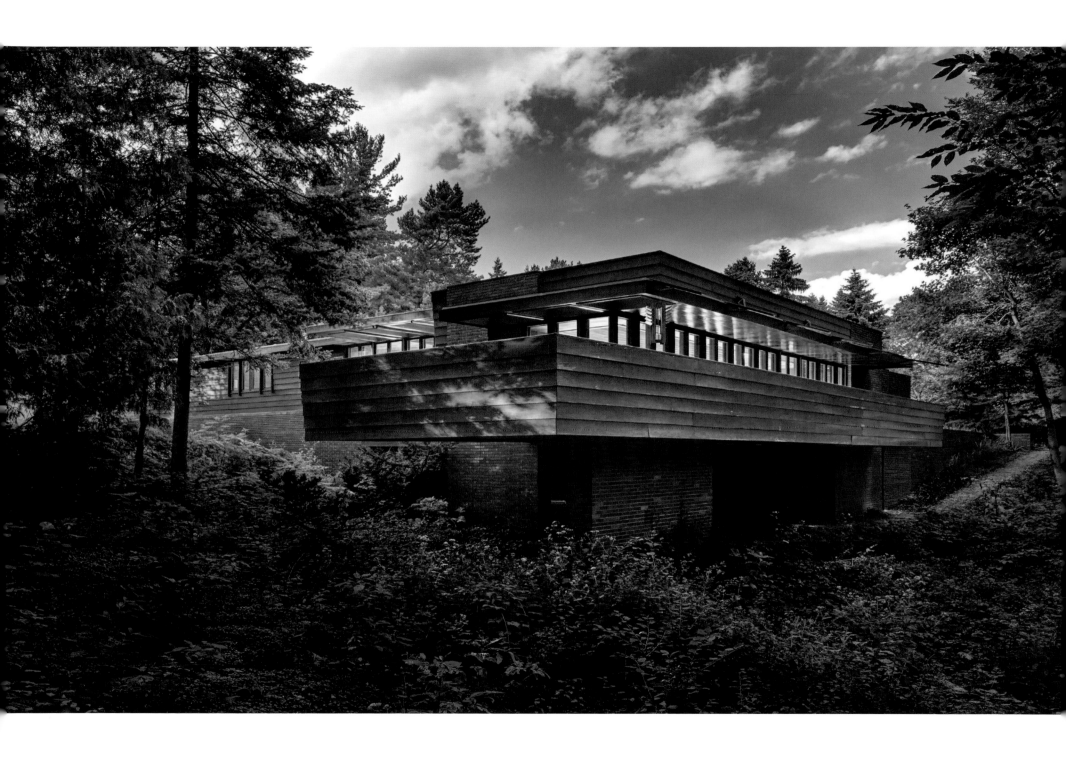

Affleck house with cantilevered balcony over ravine and stream bed.

Living room and loggia.

Dressing table in master bedroom.

MELVYN MAXWELL AND SARA SMITH HOUSE

FRANK LLOYD WRIGHT, 1949-50

BLOOMFIELD HILLS.

The Melvyn Maxwell and Sara (Stein) Smith House is a one-story, flat-roofed, L-shaped house of approximately eighteen hundred square feet sited on a three-acre, gently rolling site in Bloomfield Hills. Designed by Frank Lloyd Wright, the house possesses many of Wright's Usonian House characteristics, including connection to the topography and landscape, interplay between the interior and exterior spaces, strong horizontal emphasis created with the flat roof and dramatic overhangs, and central core consisting of the fireplace and kitchen from which the compact open floor plan radiates outward. The Smiths dubbed their house "My Haven" and Wright referred to it as "my little gem" in his correspondence with the Smiths.

Melvin Maxwell Smith first became familiar with Wright's work while taking an art and architectural survey course at Wayne State University in 1939. So taken by Wright's work, he vowed at that time that someday he would own a Wright-designed house. Smith married Sara Stein in 1941 and together they took a trip to Taliesin in Spring Green, Wisconsin. Since they were both teachers on a limited budget, they asked Wright if he could design a house to be built for five thousand dollars. Wright advised them to find a site first, but their plans were interrupted by the war.

As soon as Mr. Smith got out of the service, he went searching for a site for a new house and found an undeveloped, three-acre parcel in Bloomfield Township. He purchased the site in 1946 and immediately notified Wright, who delivered the plans in 1947. At first, Smith was discouraged, thinking he could never afford to build such a house. Wright encouraged him to act as the general contractor and get materials and labor at a discount. Smith organized friends, relatives, and tradespeople to assist with the labor. Construction on the house began in 1949 and was completed in 1950. Smith oversaw and documented every step of the construction process, from laying the foundation to installing the roofing.

The house is situated to provide privacy from the street, with the living areas opening to the outdoors and beauty of the site. The simple and unassuming entry leads to a low narrow entry passage that expands into the living area, sunken a few steps down. The living room, featuring built-in seating along the north wall and floor-to-ceiling windows along the south wall, radiates from the massive brick fireplace. The bedroom wing contains two bedrooms, two bathrooms, and a study. Pertinent details include the tinted concrete floor, which provides radiant heating, and the ceilings, walls, and trim, which use tidewater cypress.

Wright had great admiration for the Smiths, and he visited the house on three occasions: 1951, 1953, and 1957. In 1957 landscape architect Thomas Church visited the house and provided a landscape plan for a modest fee. The house was expanded in 1968 under the direction of William Wesley Peters, chief architect at the Frank Lloyd Wright Foundation, with the addition of a garden room at the corner of the L and a south terrace extending outward.

The house would become a showcase of art as well as architecture. Over the years, the Smiths amassed an impressive art collection, with the majority of the works by artists associated with nearby Cranbrook Academy of Art. Today, the Smith House is administered by the Cranbrook Educational Community and is open for scheduled tours.

The Melvyn Maxwell and Sara Smith House was listed in the National Register of Historic Places in March 1997.

LOUIS AND JOSEPHINE
ASHMUN HOUSE

ALDEN B. DOW, 1951

MIDLAND.

The Ashmun House is an elegant and elaborate A-frame structure set in a small clearing in a dense woods. Its deceptive simplicity belies the richness and beauty of the interior. The large wooden roof beams rise from steel anchors set in concrete at the ground level to the soaring ridge of the gable roof. Glass placed between the beams acts as windows on the first level and as ridge-line skylights bringing daylight into the suspended second floor. The A-profile of the front façade contrasts with an offset flat-roofed, rectangular entrance vestibule with the front wall continuing beyond the A-frame as a sidewall to the garage. The floor plan is based on an eight-foot-by-eight-foot module, with the large wood beams set at a forty-five degree angle to form the roof. The upper floor gallery is suspended cradle-like from the roof beams. The in-line floor plan was originally seventy-one feet in length, but was expanded with a 1989 rear extension addition, bringing the total length to one hundred twenty-one feet.

Josephine Griswold, a long-time Midland resident who married Louis H. Ashmun, an engineer at Dow Chemical Company, was instrumental in developing the house. Josephine's mother, Helen, was the sister of Herbert H. Dow, the founder of Dow Chemical Company, and her father, Thomas Griswold Jr., also an engineer, was the second person hired to work at the nascent chemical company in 1897. Music was an important part of Josephine's life, and she became a church organist at age eleven and played in local churches more than forty years.

So when Josephine Ashmun asked her cousin Alden B. Dow to design a house for Louis and herself, she reportedly requested only one thing, a place for her grand piano. Dow accommodated that request by making the brick floor front entry extend into the living room, forming a stage for the piano with the living room two steps below. This provides a wonderful entry sequence, as the house expands with the soaring, sloped wood walls/ceilings, suspended balcony, massive brick fireplace, and light from the side windows. The living area functions as a small concert hall--with wonderful acoustics inside the A-frame design--for listeners seated in the living room and balcony above. With all wood exposed in the interior, Josephine and Dow affectionately referred to the house as the "Timber Teepee."

Midland-based architect Alden B. Dow had a long career designing more than seventy residences, a dozen churches, and numerous schools, civic centers, art centers, and commercial buildings. Although his work was concentrated in Midland and elsewhere in Michigan, it was discussed and praised in leading architectural journals, bringing him international recognition. Born in Midland, he was the son of Herbert H. Dow, the founder of Dow Chemical Company. After three years studying chemical engineering at the University of Michigan, Dow transferred into the architecture program at Columbia University. He graduated from Columbia in 1930 and returned to Midland, where he established his own practice after becoming licensed in 1933. Still eager to sharpen his architectural skills, he and his wife, Vada, went to Spring Green, Wisconsin, in 1933 to participate in Frank Lloyd Wright's newly created apprenticeship program for architects at Taliesin. Alden and Vada were members of the first year's group of Taliesin apprentices, but only remained there for six months before returning to Midland. Dow was influenced by Wright, but his work is by no means derivative.

The Ashmun House is the only A-frame structure Dow designed that was actually built. He later experimented with the A-frame format by expanding it to a W-frame for a northern Michigan summer residence that was never constructed. Dow reportedly received more inquiries about the Ashmun House than any of his other designs.

Living room with suspended balcony.

WILLIAM AND MARY PALMER HOUSE

FRANK LLOYD WRIGHT, 1950-51

ANN ARBOR.

The Palmer House is one of the finest late works of Frank Lloyd Wright. It is considered one of the best of a series of Wright-designed houses based on an equilateral triangle module. The house, with its long, broad, hipped-roof and deep overhangs, is tucked into a gently rolling hillside surrounded by lush garden landscaping. The multilevel house rests on a red-tinted concrete pad with walls finished in brick with clear-grained cypress trim.(The brick is known as "Cranbrook brick" because it is the same brick used by architect Eliel Saarinen in the construction of Cranbrook in Bloomfield Hills.) A window band encircles the house and full-height glass doors open to terraces that extend the living area to the outside. Shallow stairs rise from the carport and parking area to the front door and a low-ceilinged entry hall with three wings radiating outward.

William B. Palmer earned his bachelor's and master's degrees in economics at the University of Michigan and then went on to teach in the university's economics program, retiring in 1976. In 1937, he married Mary Wharton Shuford, who earned her bachelor of music degree from the University of Michigan's School of Music that same year. The Palmers first lived in a remodeled farmhouse on Geddes Road in Ann Arbor, where they had two children, before deciding to build a house of their own.

In 1949, the Palmers bought two lots close to their home in the newly subdivided area north of Geddes Road, adding an adjacent lot in 1955. In the meantime, Mrs. Palmer began educating herself on residential architecture by reading books from the university's College of Architecture. She soon became an enthusiastic follower of Wright's philosophy. A visit to Wright's 1941 Affleck House in Bloomfield Hills convinced the Palmers to ask Wright to design a home for them. Prepared with topographical maps, photographs of the site, and a letter outlining the family's requirements for a house, they met with Wright in May 1950, and he agreed to design their house. Wright was already active in the region. Besides having two other clients in Ann Arbor (though their house plans were never executed), Wright also lectured in the architecture programs at both the University of Michigan and Cranbrook. In the fall of 1950 the Palmers traveled to Taliesin in Spring Green, Wisconsin, to pick up the plans for the house. They engaged Erwin Neithammer of Ann Arbor to build the house with construction beginning that fall and ending in December 1951.

Wright had used the equilateral triangle as a planning module as early as 1927 in the Ocatillo Desert Camp in Arizona. The house exemplifies Wright's organic architecture, seemingly growing out of the natural terrain with low broad overhangs providing a strong sense of shelter. A substantial fireplace and chimney anchor the center of the house with open ceilings following the rooflines. Living spaces flow together and extend to the exterior with terraces and views. The open interior is fitted with Wright-designed furniture and built-in cabinetry. Three bedrooms and a study are up a few steps from the living area off the hallway or gallery, which is lined with bookshelves.

While Wright included brick retaining walls to help set the house into the hillside, the Palmers developed the site with extensive landscaping with two distinct zones. The first, adjacent to the back of the house, is a three-tiered flat grassy terrace area leading away from the house. The second is the copse, a native overstory of trees complemented by ornamental plantings of groundcover and flowering shrubs with curvilinear pathways.

Michigan is fortunate to have the third largest collection of Wright-designed buildings in the country. With only one residence and several summer homes from his early Prairie style period, most Wright homes in Michigan are from his Usonian and late periods. The Palmer House is considered one of Wright's finest houses from his late period. The Palmers lived in the house for over 45 years and kept it meticulously maintained, as have the current owners.

The William and Mary Palmer House was listed in the National Register of Historic Places in March 1999.

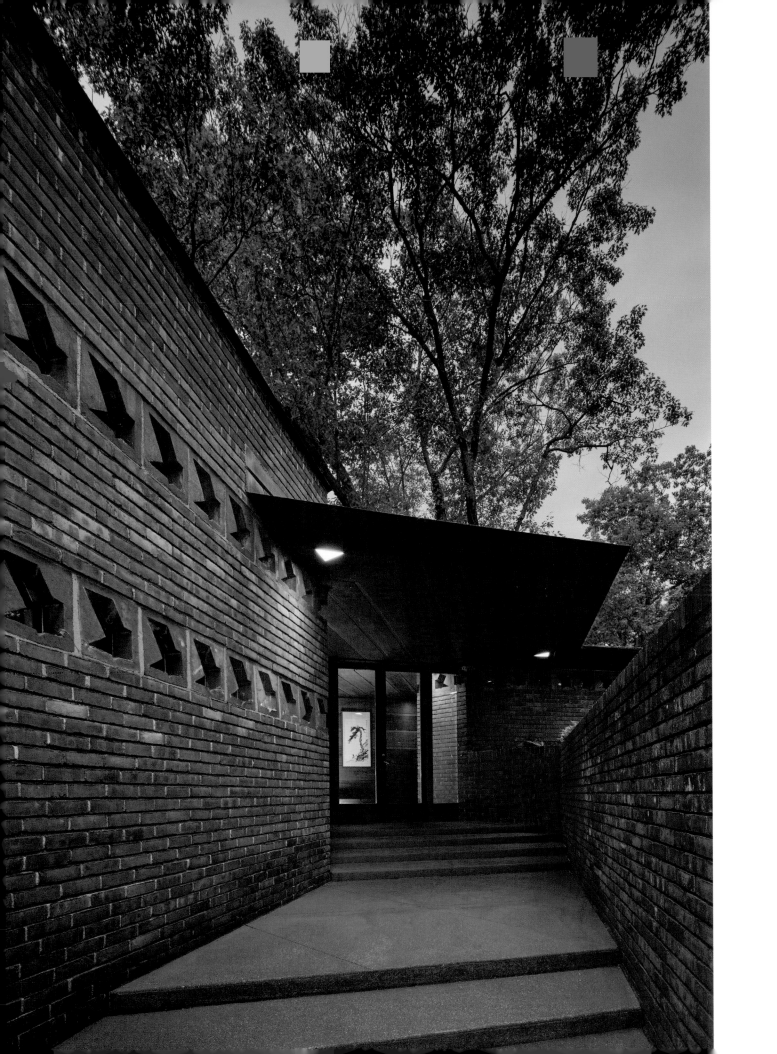

JOHN AND KATHLEEN McLUCAS HOUSE

ALEXANDER GIRARD, 1950

GROSSE POINTE.

John "Jack" Nichols McLucas came to Detroit in 1945 to accept the position of vice president of the National Bank of Detroit. By the end of 1946, he had married Kathleen "Kitty" Smith, adopted a daughter, Virginia "Jinx," and moved the family to Grosse Pointe, Michigan. The McLucases joined prominent clubs like the Detroit Athletic Club, Country Club of Detroit, Grosse Pointe Hunt Club and Junior League of Detroit. They probably met Alexander and Susan Girard through social connections, though they lived on the same street.

Alexander Girard, known to friends as "Sandro," was an influential Modern designer of extraordinary depth and breadth. He is perhaps best known for his boldly colored textiles, furnishings, and graphics designed for the Herman Miller Furniture Company of Zeeland, Michigan, where he worked closely with George Nelson, Charles and Ray Eames, and others. His work reflects the folk art and bright colors he loved. Born in New York in 1907, he was raised in Florence, Italy, where his Italian father was a master woodworker and collector of fine arts and antiques. Girard graduated with honors from the Royal Institute of British Architects in London and later studied design in Rome. Before moving to Michigan in 1937, he worked in New York City and was a member of the Architectural League of New York and the American Institute of Decorators.

Girard became the chief designer for the Detroit-based radio manufacturer Detrola in 1943, designing radios and turntables. He eventually redesigned the company's offices and plant facilities. There, he met Charles Eames, who was designing molded plywood radio cabinets for Detrola, and the two became lifelong friends and colleagues. Girard opened his own design studio in Grosse Pointe in 1947. He showcased modern home furnishings in a major exhibition titled For Modern Living that he curated for the Detroit Institute of Arts in 1949. The exhibition received national acclaim and brought the work of many modern designers to the attention of the general public.

Girard collaborated with other Michigan-based architects of note, including Eero Saarinen and Minoru Yamasaki. He worked with Saarinen on the interiors of the Gateway Arch in Saint Louis, Missouri, the John Deere World Headquarters in Moline, Illinois; the General Motors Technical Center in Warren, Michigan; and the Irwin Miller House in Columbus, Indiana. He began working with Herman Miller in 1952 as a textile designer and remained with the company until 1973, designing furniture, graphics, and showrooms as well as fabrics. In addition to his work for Herman Miller, he designed innovative interiors such as La Fonda del Sol restaurant in New York City in 1960. He was responsible for the complete redesign of interiors for Braniff International Airways in 1965.

The McLucas House was one of four private residences Girard designed in Grosse Pointe in the years 1947-51, including his own home. (All but the McLucas House have been demolished.) Girard's earliest surviving drawings for the McLucas House date to December 1949, a time when he was involved with several collaborative projects with Eero Saarinen and Charles Eames. The house is designed around a central, open-air atrium. Accented with primary colored glazed brick walls that run from the exterior into the interior, the atrium connects the indoors with the outdoors. Its colored glazed brick are identical to those expressly developed for the General Motors Technical Center, designed by Saarinen around the same time. Girard's role as design and color consultant for the Technical Center--and his close friendship with Saarinen--may explain Girard's access to the Technical Center's unique bricks, which were developed in partnership with Cranbrook ceramic artists and the ceramic scientists in GM's spark plug division.

The open floor plan, large expanses of glass, and partition walls running from interior through to the exterior all reflect the tenets of good design Girard promoted as curator of the For Modern Living exhibition. The open web steel ceiling joists he employed in the living room, similar to those used by his friends and colleagues Charles and Ray Eames in the Case Study House, their own residence in Pacific Palisades, California, add to the open quality and lightness of the McLucas House.

The current owners are restoring the house with textile designer Ruth Adler Schnee as design consultant. Schnee, a graduate of Cranbrook, worked with Saarinen, Yamasaki, and other noted midcentury architects. Her designs are still being produced by Knoll and Anzea Textiles.

Glazed brick wall leading
from bedroom hallway to
exterior courtyard.

Above, Bedroom hallway with art print by Susan Skarsgard.

Left, Front entry.
Right, View from rear yard.

RICHARD AND FLORENCE
CRANE HOUSE

ROBERT C. METCALF, 1954

ANN ARBOR.

Ann Arbor, the home of the University of Michigan's Taubman College of Architecture and Urban Planning, has a wealth of modern residential architecture designed by the college's faculty members. Constructed primarily between 1945 and 1970, they constitute one of the largest collections of modern residences in Michigan. The Richard and Florence Crane House, designed by Robert C. Metcalf, is a distinguished example.

The architecture program at the University of Michigan was established in in 1907 with Emil Lorch as the first dean. Lorch was a Detroit native who had worked as an instructor at the Art Institute of Chicago at the turn of the century. This was the period when Frank Lloyd Wright and the Prairie School architects were searching for a new form of architecture education to challenge traditional Beaux Arts methods and encourage young architects to incorporate new materials and modern design concepts in their work. To that end, Lorch adapted a progressive art education method called Pure Design to the architecture program he established at the University of Michigan, making it one of the nation's first architectural programs to begin teaching modern design philosophies.

Lorch invited George Brigham, an architect designing historic revival homes in Southern California, to teach at the University of Michigan in 1930. Brigham soon became a proponent of modern design, and designed what is considered to be the first modern house in Ann Arbor in 1935. Robert Metcalf was a student of Brigham's and served as his chief draftsman from 1948-52, working on approximately thirty residential projects in the region. Metcalf started his own architectural practice in 1953 and the Crane House was his first independent commission.

Like Metcalf, the Cranes were also associated with the university. Richard Crane was a professor of physics and the inventor of the Race Track Synchrotron, an early particle accelerator. As a distinguished experimental physicist, he maintained contact with such notable scientists as Albert Einstein, Niels Bohr, and Edwin Hubble, and was awarded the National Medal of Science by President Ronald Reagan. Florence Crane was a community leader and political activist. She completed two terms on the Ann Arbor City Council, was the first woman on the board of National Bank and Trust, and served seventeen years on the Michigan State Corrections Commission.

Metcalf designed a house to fit the Cranes' needs and lifestyle. The house accommodated three teenage children, quiet space for the parent's active intellectual lives, and a workspace for Richard Crane's experiments. The house was also configured for hosting and entertaining. To take full advantage of natural light, Metcalf designed the house with south-facing windows and made use of wide overhangs above the expansive windows to admit sunlight during the winter and provide shade in the summer. The house is built into the hillside, exposing two full stories on the front with the upper level at ground level in the back. Its lightweight steel joist construction provides large open rooms and enables rooms to flow from one to another.

Following the Crane House commission and the completion of his own house with his wife Bettie in 1954, Robert Metcalf went on to design close to seventy houses in Ann Arbor. His houses are known for careful attention to detail and for siting to maximize light and views. Over the course of his career, Metcalf produced over 150 building projects in Michigan and Ohio. He worked with Tivadar Balogh and William Werner, both University of Michigan alumni and instructors in the College of Architecture and Urban Design, and other architects.

Metcalf became a faculty member at the university's College of Architecture and Urban Design in 1955. Holding the position of chairman from 1968 to 1974 and dean from 1974 until 1991, he retired with emeritus status. He was a member of the College of Fellows of the American Institute of Architects and received the President's Lifetime Achievement Award from AIA Michigan in 1999 as well as numerous awards for his work.

Left, Front entry hall with stairs up to main living level.
Right, Master bedroom.

WILLIAM AND ELIZABETH MUSCHENHEIM HOUSE

WILLIAM MUSCHENHEIM, 1954

ANN ARBOR.

William Muschenheim, a native of New York City whose family owned the Astor Hotel, attended Williams College and the Massachusetts Institute of Technology before receiving his master of architecture degree from the Behrens Master School of Architecture, Academy of Fine Arts, in Vienna, Austria (1925-1929). Deeply affected by a short visit to the Bauhaus, he formed a lifelong commitment to a Modernist approach to architecture, and become a member of the Congrès Internationaux d'Architecture Moderne (CIAM), a European organization founded in 1928 to promote Modern architecture. He began working in the New York office of architect Joseph Urban in 1929, where he was involved in the design of the futuristic, Art Deco-style auditorium at the New York School of Social Research. (When Urban was selected as the Director of Exterior Color for the 1933 Century of Progress International Exhibition in Chicago, Muschenheim was named the project's lead colorist.) His striking group of beach houses for the Muschenheim family in the Hamptons earned him inclusion in Philip Johnson's Rejected Architects exhibition, one of the first to showcase the International Style in America, in 1931.

In 1934, Muschenheim established his own architectural practice and spent the next sixteen years designing residences on Long Island, winning recognition as the architect of some of the region's earliest Modern structures, and in New York. Upon the recommendation of his friend Knud Londberg-Holm, he was invited to join the faculty of the University of Michigan's College of Architecture and Urban Design in 1950, a time of directional change for the school. Along with architects Ted Larson and Walter Sanders, Muschenheim led a reorganization of the architectural program to focus on design and research.

One of many architecture faculty members who designed homes for themselves, their colleagues, and others throughout the city of Ann Arbor (their work has recently become known as the Ann Arbor School) Muschenheim designed and built his split three-level family home in the Ann Arbor Hills neighborhood in 1954. The house is rectangular in plan, rising up a slight hillside with a long sloping roof. Its concrete block and lightweight prefabricated steel structural system is generally reserved for use in industrial projects. The rear facade is composed of large expanses of windows and strategically placed highlights of primary color.

The William and Elizabeth Muschenheim House was listed in the National Register of Historic Places in December 2016.

Living room and dining area.

GENERAL MOTORS TECHNICAL CENTER

EERO SAARINEN, 1949-56

WARREN.

The General Motors Technical Center was embraced around the world as the embodiment of the spirit of prosperity, modernity, and futurism in post-World War II America, a groundbreaking work that brought its architect, Eero Saarinen, international recognition. A campus of buildings grouped by function surrounding a man-made lake in the Detroit suburb of Warren, the Center was created as the main facility for advanced research, engineering, and product design for General Motors, one of the world's largest corporations, and continues in that role today. The complex covers nearly a square mile.

Eero Saarinen was born in Finland and followed in the footsteps of his father Eliel Saarinen in becoming an architect. Showing an early propensity for drawing, he began his education at his father's desk in Cranbrook. Eliel Saarinen initially came to Michigan to teach at the University of Michigan, and then to design the campus of Cranbrook Academy of Art and help develop its educational curriculum. Eero studied architecture at Yale University and returned to Bloomfield Hills upon graduation to join his father's architectural practice, Saarinen and Swanson, and to teach at Cranbrook.

The initial planning and design for the project took place in 1944-45 with Eliel Saarinen as the design leader at Saarinen and Swanson. Material and funding shortages coupled with a major strike by the United Auto Workers placed the project on hold. While the project resumed in 1949, Eliel Saarinen died in 1950. Harley Earl, head of design at General Motors, convinced the company board to retain the relatively unknown younger Saarinen to complete the project. Under the firm name of Eero Saarinen and Associates, Saarinen redesigned his father's original plan and collaborated with other design firms and General Motors designers to complete the project. Smith Hinchman & Grylls of Detroit served as project engineers and produced working drawings. Thomas D. Church developed the landscape plan, and landscape architect Edward A. Eichstedt developed specific planting lists and supervised the landscape development.

The historic campus consists of five major building groups arranged in an orthogonal pattern on three sides of a central, rectangular artificial lake. The lake provides the campus with its main visual focal point and emphasizes the horizontality and panoramic, automobile scale of the design. Its fourth side, containing a grid of trees, is open and serves as the main entrance to the campus. An elegant and dramatic, stainless steel-sheathed water tower adds a vertical sculptural element at one corner of the lake and serves as a counterpoint to the aluminum-clad dome of the Styling Auditorium at the opposite corner. There are two water fountains; one consists of two rows of vertical jets that provide a wall of water at the entrance, and the other is a design by Alexander Calder that plays a pattern of sequenced water dances.

The five groupings of buildings surrounding the lake are low-rise rectangular, flat roofed, curtained-walled structures that display solid, colored glazed brick end walls. Each has a projecting entrance canopy of unique design. The colored glazed brick was developed at Cranbrook in consultation with the General Motors spark plug group. Lobbies have floor-to-ceiling glass windows, some set in movable panels to facilitate the movement of automobiles into the lobbies for display. The interior lobbies are each different, with dramatic stairways and finish treatments.

The General Motors Technical Center was listed in the National Register of Historic Places in March 2000 and listed as a National Historic Landmark in August 2014.

Staircase in the Styling (Design) Building lobby.

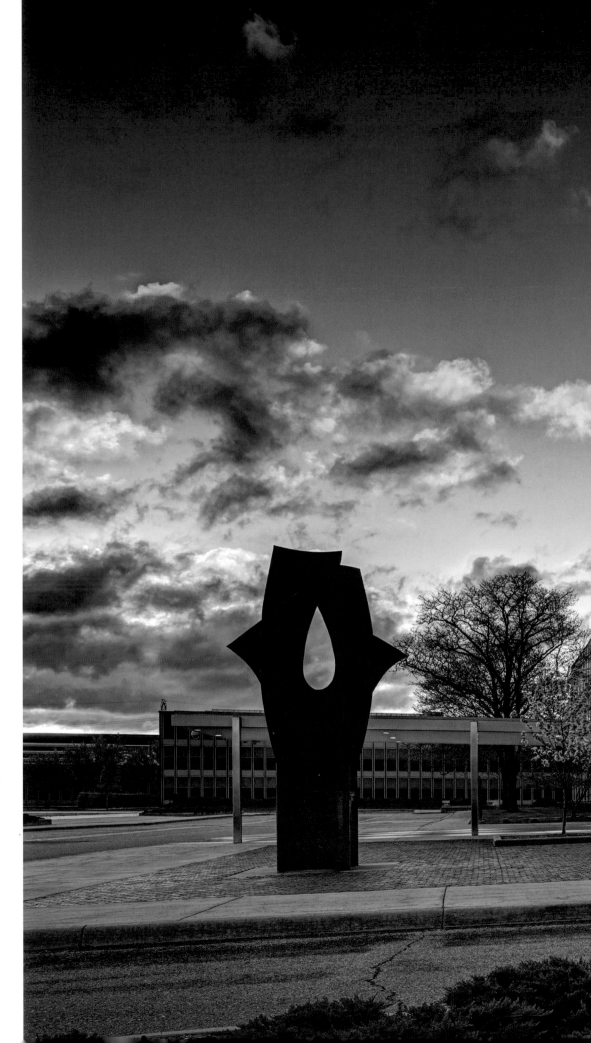

*Styling (Design) Building
with Bird in Flight sculpture
by Antoine Pevsner.*

Left, Styling (Design) Building lobby with 1951 Le Sabre concept car. Above, Reception 'teacup" desk in Styling (Design) Building lobby.

Above, Styling (Design) Building lobby.
Right, General Motors Technical Center surrounding a man-made lake.

Styling (Design) Auditorium.

Staircase in Research Building lobby.

DOROTHY
TURKEL HOUSE

FRANK LLOYD WRIGHT, 1956-57

DETROIT.

The Turkel House is a late work of architect Frank Lloyd Wright and is the only Wright-designed house in Detroit. A two-story building with an L-shaped plan, it is an example of Wright's Usonian Automatic genre of houses. These houses utilize a technique of concrete block construction comprising specially made blocks dry-laid with horizontal and vertical reinforcement rods placed in channels and filled with concrete to bind the components together.

In 1936, Frank Lloyd Wright developed his original concept for a low-cost house he termed Usonian. A Usonian House was designed to be built on a concrete slab with no basement or attic, and little ornamentation. Plans were compact and designed for simple modern living. In his late period, Wright continued to develop his Usonian concepts and incorporated its ideals into larger houses such as the Palmer House of 1950-51 in Ann Arbor and the Turkel House.

Wright first experimented with the use of decorative concrete blocks on four homes in Los Angeles in the 1920s. He coined the term Usonian Automatic in the early 1950s to describe a Usonian type house built of inexpensive concrete blocks that could be assembled in a variety of ways. Wright encouraged homeowners to build the Usonian Automatic houses themselves with concrete blocks formed on site. Examples of owner-built houses built to Wright's plans in Michigan can be found in Parkwyn Village in Kalamazoo and The Acres outside Galesburg, two Wright Usonian neighborhoods. The Turkel House differs from other Wright Usonian Automatic Houses in a number of ways. It is a two-story house, it is the work of a contractor rather than a homeowner, and it employs square blocks that reflect the scale of the house. Many different block forms were required, including a special fascia block and a fascia corner block used only for that purpose. The living room, which Wright called a music room, is a full two stories in height and has pierced, light-admitting blocks on two sides that create a unique two-story corner of small square windows, producing wonderful light patterns as the daylight changes through a day.

Dorothy Turkel's father had become wealthy by developing and managing parking lots in the early years as automobiles reshaped cities across the nation. Ms. Turkel married Henry Turkel, a physician, and they lived in Detroit's Boston-Edison neighborhood with their four children. Intrigued by contemporary organic architecture, she asked Frank Lloyd Wright to design a home for the family in Detroit soon after reading his book, The Natural House. In a letter she wrote to Wright in January 1954, she recounted her vision for a new house in the fashionable Palmer Woods neighborhood, and asked Wright if he would design such a house.

Within three months she had blueprints in hand. The original plan was an in-line, two-story version of Wright's Usonian concept with Ms. Turkel's study, the master bedroom, and three other bedrooms, plus three bathrooms and a balcony fitting over the lower level workspace/kitchen, dining area, and laundry/utility rooms in an in-line configuration opening to a terrace. The end of the in-line plan was the two-story living room, which Wright labeled the music room on the plans, overlooked by a second floor balcony. Six months into the planning Mrs. Turkel wrote to Wright saying she needed another bedroom, and a leg was added to the plan, creating the L-shaped floor plan. As built, the leg was shortened, with a playroom on the main level and a boy's bedroom and maid's room on the second floor. Robert Pond supervised construction from drawings prepared by John Howe in Wright's office. In the two years required to complete the house, the couple divorced, and Ms. Turkel moved into the house with the four children in February 1958. She remained there until 1978.

The current owners have completed an extensive and faithful restoration of the house utilizing original plans and Turkel family photographs to guide them.

Entry from patio area.

Above, Second floor balcony overlooking patio area,
Right, Family/playroom.

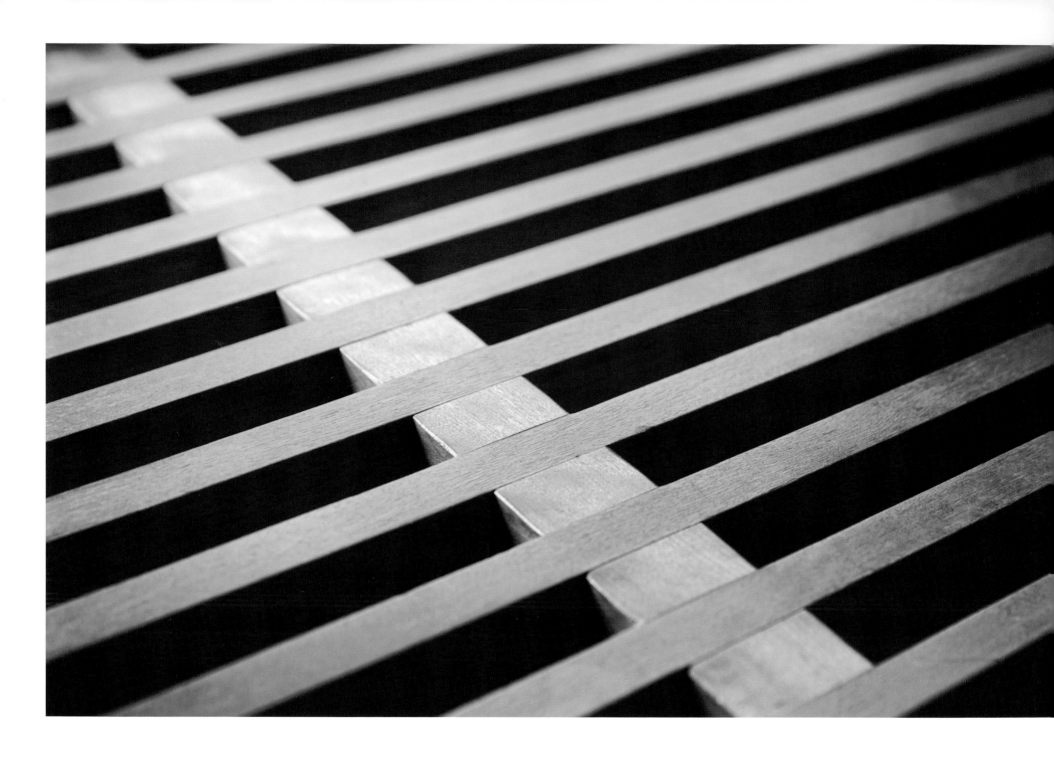

Page 126, Detail of a Nelson-designed bench.
Left, Galley kitchen.
Bottom left, Detail of speaker system and
Nelson-designed clock.

Page 132, Living room of a
two-story townhouse residence.
Left, Kitchen of a two-story
townhouse residence.

Lafayette Towers

Pavilion Tower, second tall building from the left, and Lafayette Towers on the right, with Garden-court and Townhouse residences among the trees.

137

HERMAN MILLER
MAIN SITE BUILDING

GEORGE NELSON, 1958;
A. QUINCY JONES, 1970

ZEELAND.

D. J. (Dirk Jan) DePree started his career in the West Michigan furniture industry in 1908 as a clerk for the Star Furniture Company in Zeeland. By 1919 he had risen to president of the company. At that time West Michigan, anchored by Grand Rapids, was known as the furniture capital of America. DePree convinced his father-in-law, Herman Miller, to purchase a majority of shares in the company in 1923, and DePree renamed the company after him as a tribute. A producer of conventional, historically inspired furniture at the time, Herman Miller changed its direction due to a chance meeting between DePree and industrial designer Gilbert Rohde. Rohde convinced DePree that the company's reproduction furniture was neither honest nor authentic. DePree gave Rohde an opportunity to design a line of modern furniture that was completed in time for display in a model home at the Century of Progress Exposition of 1933 in Chicago. The furniture's success with the general public led DePree to hire Rohde as the director of design for Herman Miller. Because DePree boldly committed the company to produce only innovative modern furniture, Rohde's new, streamlined furniture was completely free of historic references.

Rohde's untimely death in 1944 left DePree and the Herman Miller furniture company in search of a new design director. The publication of an article by George Nelson in Life magazine on his innovative Storage Wall designs caught DePree's attention, and lead to a twenty-seven-year career for Nelson as the director of design for Herman Miller–as well as a life-long friendship between the two men. Nelson was responsible for inviting other talented designers to contribute to Herman Miller's portfolio of designs for production, including Charles and Ray Eames, Isamu Noguchi, Alexander Girard and Robert Propst. The result was some of the most iconic modern furniture ever mass-produced. Herman Miller's tradition of commissioning multiple designers continues to this day.

In the mid-1950s, facing the need to consolidate manufacturing operations and the prospect of sales growth for the popular furniture designed by Nelson, the Eameses, and others, Herman Miller purchased open farmland outside of Zeeland for new facilities. Nelson's design firm, George Nelson Associates, designed the first building on the site as well as the master plan, with Gordon Chadwick serving as team leader. The first section, now known as Building 8-East, opened in 1958. The one-story brick building fit well on the flat site and was designed to accommodate future expansion. Access to daylight, covered truck docks, and common finishes and furniture for both office and plant areas were among the company's progressive requirements for the mixed office and manufacturing facility.

Chadwick's five-building master plan guided facility development at Herman Miller for over a decade, and introduced a unique futuristic-looking and sculptural raised walkway that provides access and views into manufacturing areas. California architect A. Quincy Jones developed a new master plan for the complex in 1970 that led to expansions including an Energy Center, a Computer Center, and the conversion of eighty-eight thousand square feet of manufacturing space to office use. In the mid-1980s, the Minneapolis architectural firm of Meyer, Scherer, and Rockcastle completed a major renovation of the office area with the goal of displaying the company's system furniture to best advantage.

Herman Miller revolutionized office environments worldwide with the development of system or modular furniture and office environments. Graphic artist and sculptor Robert Probst became president of the Herman Miller Research Corporation in 1960, and together with George Nelson developed Action Office, a system of movable and interchangeable office furniture and components that was introduced in 1968. As the world's first open office system, Action Office revolutionized the office furniture industry and made Herman Miller a Fortune 500 Company.

Today, Herman Miller continues to be a leader in production of office systems as office environments continue to evolve in terms of efficiency, creativity, and technology. Its classic lines of residential furniture remain in production, with some designs having never ceased production and others being periodically reintroduced, along with new designs by today's talented designers. The original Zeeland complex continues to serve as a showcase for Herman Miller products, demonstrating the company's progressive attitudes about people, architecture, and their interaction. Of course, the 121-acre Main Site campus is now just one of numerous Herman Miller facilities in the Zeeland and Holland areas of West Michigan and around the world.

"The Spine," a second
floor balcony walk linking
areas of the complex.

Main entrance.

Left, "The Spine" continues as an overhead connector between buildings.

Addition by A. Quincy Jones.

McGREGOR
MEMORIAL
CONFERENCE
CENTER

MINORU YAMASAKI, 1958

DETROIT.

The McGregor Memorial Conference Center on the campus of Wayne State University in Detroit was a seminal work for architect Minoru Yamasaki. Completed in 1957, it heralded a significant change in his architectural philosophy, ushering in a new type of modern architecture that became known as New Formalism.

In the early 1950s, Yamaskai was a partner in the firm of Leinweber, Yamasaki & Hellmuth, dividing his time between the firm's offices in St. Louis and Detroit, working on such major projects as Lambert-St. Louis Airport and the Pruitt-Igoe urban renewal housing project in St. Louis, and developing a master plan for the Gratiot Redevelopment Area, a major urban renewal project in Detroit. The stress of balancing work, family, and travel took a toll on Yamasaki's health, and the decision was made to split the firm in two. Yamasaki established an office in Detroit with Joseph Leinweber, while George Hellmuth remained in St. Louis and founded Hellmuth, Obata + Kassabaum (now known as HOK).

In 1955 Yamasaki & Leinweber received the commission to design the United States Consulate in Kobe, Japan, which enabled Yamasaki to journey overseas. As his health was still fragile, he took time off to travel around the world. This life-changing experience exposed him to the regional architecture of Europe, India, and Southeast Asia. As he recalled, "This gave me the opportunity to collect my thoughts about the kind of design I was doing. I found myself strongly affected by the humanistic qualities of historical buildings, qualities that I had not encountered in contemporary structures." Although Yamasaki had been a proponent of the International Style, after traveling abroad he began searching for a way to incorporate a more human element into the International Style, which he increasingly saw as sterile, functional architecture. The words he used most often to describe what he sought were "surprise," "serenity," and "delight."

In 1954 the McGregor Fund in Detroit decided to build a community conference center to commemorate its founders on the edge of the Wayne State University campus in downtown Detroit. The McGregor Memorial Conference Center was to serve as a bridge between the city and the campus. Yamasaki's design for the Center is the first incarnation of his vision for a new architecture.

The building sits on an elevated plinth wrapped on two sides by a sunken reflecting pool and sculpture garden. On the exterior, the north and south elevations are smooth planes of warm travertine marble bisected by a two-story glass atrium wall. Decorative aluminum screens designed by sculptor Lee du Sell cover the entry doors at both ends. The east and west elevations are distinguished by triangular protrusions on columns faced with white St. Cloud marble that jet out at second floor and roof levels. Inside, the system of triangular protrusions on columns is repeated in the lobby atrium. The atrium soars upward like a cathedral with the bold diamond pattern skylight ceiling filling the lobby with a play of light and shadow. The simple interior is warmed by materials like travertine, white marble, and teak, and features interior furnishings designed by Yamasaki in collaboration with Florence Schust Knoll (now Florence Knoll Bassett) and the Knoll Planning Group.

The McGregor Memorial Conference Center was the first of four buildings that Yamasaki designed for the Wayne State University campus, as part of a larger campus plan he developed for the University as they looked to stay in Detroit rather than move to the suburbs in the 1950s. Yamasaki also designed the university's College of Education (1960), Helen L. DeRoy Auditorium (1964) and Prentis Building (1964). The McGregor Memorial Conference Center received the AIA Honor Award upon its completion in 1958.

Interestingly, the reflecting pool, first used in the design of the McGregor Memorial Conference Center, became a signature feature of many Yamasaki buildings, providing a place of serenity within the hustle and bustle of the city. Pools were incorporated into the design of Yamasaki's later work including the Reynolds Metals Regional Sales Office Building (1959) in Southfield, Michigan, the Michigan Gas Company Building (1963) in Detroit, and the Helen L. DeRoy Auditorium (1962-64) at Wayne State University. The reflecting pool at the McGregor Memorial Center underwent a major restoration by Quinn Evans Architects of Ann Arbor in 2013.

The McGregor Memorial Conference Center was listed in the National Register of Historic Places in December 2010 and listed as a National Historic Landmark in February 2015.

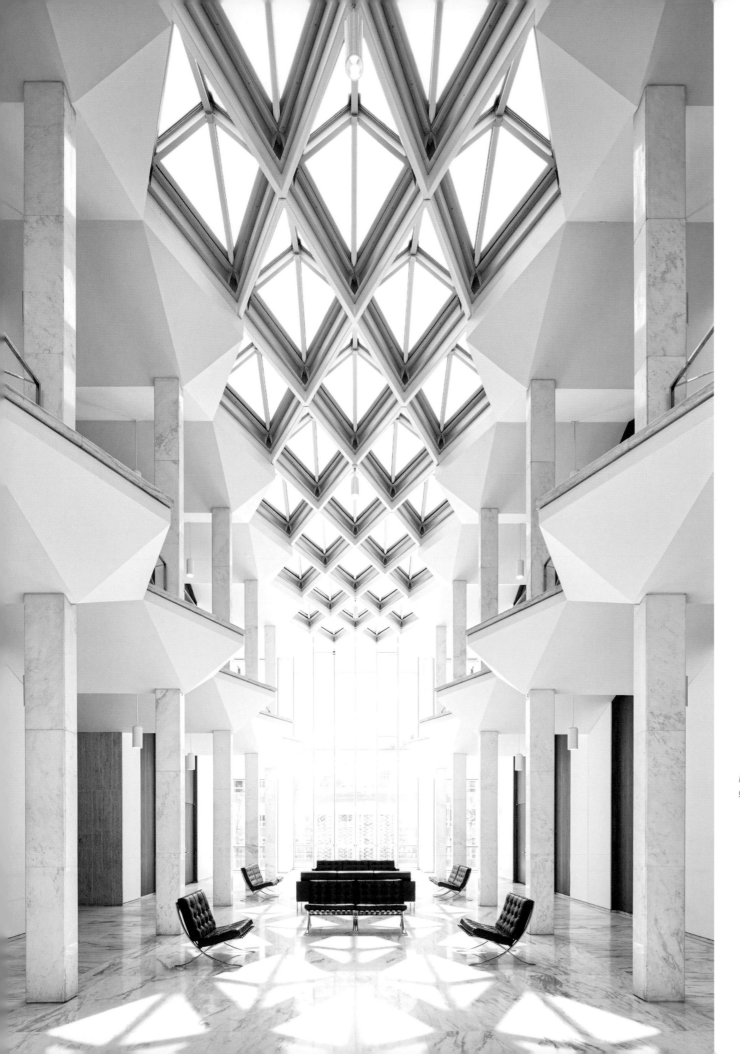

*Interior lobby/
gathering space.*

JOHN AND MARGARET RIECKER HOUSE

ALDEN B. DOW, 1961

MIDLAND.

Architect Alden B. Dow designed the Riecker House for his favorite niece Margaret Towsley Riecker, her husband John, and their two children with one stipulation: that the house be their home for life. Dow fulfilled their wish with the Riecker House. John and Margaret both grew up in Ann Arbor, went to the same high school, married in 1955, and moved to Midland in 1958. John became a successful attorney and an active volunteer and board member for numerous organizations in Midland and statewide until his death in 2008.

Margaret Riecker was the granddaughter of Herbert Dow, the founder of Dow Chemical Company. Known as "Ranny," she was an active community leader and volunteer as well as a strong believer in collaborative philanthropy. Besides earning a bachelor of arts degree from Carlton College in Northfield, Minnesota, she received honorary degrees throughout her life from such institutions as Albion College, Central Michigan University, Ferris State University, Kalamazoo College, University of Michigan, Northwood University and Michigan State University. She was a trustee of the Herbert H. and Grace A. Dow Foundation for fifty-one years, serving as president from 2000 until her death in 2014. In addition, she spent many years as a trustee of the Harry A. and Margaret D. Towsley Foundation, and held the office of vice chair of the Michigan Republican Party and a Republican National Committee member from Michigan in the 1970s. Ranny was a co-founder of the Council of Michigan Foundations, a trustee from 1974-2000, and chair from 1982-1964. She was unquestionably an important figure in Michigan's philanthropic and political circles.

Dow designed the Riecker House on a seven-foot module. It is an elegant combination of brick walls and a flat, multiple-beam roof frame exposed on the interior as an intricate module grid ceiling pattern. Main beams and cross beams interlock to create the ceiling grid while providing long spans and open spaces, with brick interior bearing walls to organize and define interior spaces. Though appearing as one level on the exterior, the incorporation of a one-step level change inside further defines spaces and provides integration with the gently sloping landscape. The front façade is an almost symmetrical composition of flat, windowless brick wall planes extending beyond the structure with the exposed-end beamed roof structure floating above clerestory windows. The central front entry is recessed and welcoming with large windows flanking the oversized door. The rear façade opens with floor-to-ceiling glass providing views to the landscape sloping down to Sturgeon Creek. Clerestory windows are placed between the beams, so the ceilings appear to float above the walls.

A screen porch was converted into a sunroom in 1965 and Dow added a study for Ranny off the master bedroom in 1967. Following damage that occurred from the historic one-hundred-year flood in 1986, the Rieckers took the opportunity to update portions of the house's interior and called upon Don Howell, president of Alden Dow's successor firm, Dow Howell Gilmore Associates, for the work. The kitchen was renovated, skylights were added to the kitchen and sunroom, and two bedrooms were combined into one for a media room. The sixty-eight-hundred-square-foot house provided a tranquil environment for family living and served the Rieckers well until Ranny's death in 2014.

Alden B. Dow was the son of Dow Chemical founder Herbert Dow and his wife Grace. Practicing in Midland, he was the architect of choice for many of Dow Chemical's management as the community of Midland grew. As a result, Midland represents a museum of Dow's work, including close to sixty homes, churches and public buildings. Dow was named Michigan's Architect Laureate in 1983.

*Left, Dow-designed garden lights,
Right, Pool and trellis outside bedroom wing.*

MICHIGAN CONSOLIDATED GAS COMPANY BUILDING

MINORU YAMASAKI, 1962-63

DETROIT.

The Michigan Consolidated Gas Company Building, located on a prominent block in Detroit between the Detroit River and the Civic Center, was developed as part of a master plan created for the city by Eero Saarinen and Associates in 1951. Built as the headquarters for Michigan Consolidated Gas Company, the twenty-eight-story building is architect Minoru Yamasaki's first skyscraper. This design led to other tall building commissions such as the Century Plaza Towers in Los Angeles, and is considered the precursor to his design for the World Trade Center in New York City.

The steel frame structure is covered in pre-cast, pre-stressed concrete panels, each weighing one ton. The concrete contains white quartz aggregate to complement the white marble of the Civic Center's showcase buildings: the City-County Building, Veteran's Memorial, and Ford Auditorium (now demolished). The use of concrete panels was meant to provide an alternative to the typical steel-framed glass curtain wall then in vogue. The building is distinguished by its forty-eight hundred windows, shaped in the form of narrow hexagons extending from floor to ceiling, rendering 50 percent of the building's exterior as glass. The windows give a sense of both intimacy and spaciousness from the interior and verticality from the exterior, offering an airy contrast to the building's heavy horizontal spans. At the top of the building, a four-story mechanical penthouse covered with a decorative metal grill has been installed to move the mechanical systems out of the basement, so parking could be incorporated under the building. At the time of the building's completion, colored lights were used to highlight a boxed cooling tower at the top.

The building sits on a marble platform that was once surrounded by a reflecting pool that held a sculpture by Giacomo Manza. The pool had gas jets that provided flame torches rising from the water. The exterior walls of the recessed lobby consist of thirty-foot panels of glass in a metal frame. The soaring two-story lobby has floors and columns covered in white marble and a ceiling of white coffered panels. Decorative aluminum X-frames designed by sculptor Lee Du Soll were placed over white ceiling panels, with each aluminum frame containing a small, centered, deep-blue light globe meant to simulate the glow of gas jets. Yamasaki designed the building in association with the Detroit firm of Smith, Hinchman & Grylls. In 1964, soon after the building's completion, he was awarded the coveted commission to design the World Trade Center. By this time, he had received commissions across the country and was featured on the cover of Time magazine for January 18, 1963.

Yamasaki came to Detroit in 1945 to work in the architectural firm of Smith, Hinchman & Grylls. Several years later, he and two colleagues established Leinweber, Yamasaki & Hellmuth with offices in St. Louis and Detroit. In 1959 he established the firm of Yamasaki & Associates in Troy, Michigan. The firm's increasing number of commissions extended its reach far beyond Detroit and Michigan. While perhaps most renowned for his design of the World Trade Center in New York, Yamasaki produced significant designs throughout the United States, as well as in India, Japan, and Saudi Arabia. Some of the firm's most notable designs include the Civil Air Terminal, in Dhahran, Saudi Arabia (1961); Michigan Consolidated Gas Company Building, in Detroit (1963); Reynolds Aluminum Building, in Southfield, Michigan (1967); the United States Pavilion for World Agriculture Fair, in New Delhi, India (1960); the Federal Science Pavilion for the Century 21 Exhibition, in Seattle, Washington (1962); the Woodrow Wilson School of Public and International Affairs at Princeton University, in Princeton, New Jersey (1961); and the Century Plaza Hotel and Towers, in Los Angeles (1966 and 1972). Yamasaki won numerous awards and honorary degrees, and his work was featured in national and international publications and exhibitions.

Viewed through "Transcending," a sculpture by David Barr on Hart Plaza.

163

The wall of buildings framing Hart Plaza envisioned
in the Detroit Riverfront plan by Eero Saarinen.

CONGREGATION SHAAREY ZEDEK SYNAGOGUE

PERCIVAL GOODMAN, 1962-63

SOUTHFIELD.

Congregation Shaarey Zedek was founded in 1861 and worshipped in several locations throughout Detroit during the late nineteenth and early twentieth centuries. By the mid-twentieth century, many members of Detroit's Jewish community had moved to the city's northern suburbs, with several congregations subsequently following their members.

In 1956, architect Percival Goodman was commissioned to design a new suburban complex for Congregation Shaarey Zedek. Goodman was a respected leading designer of Jewish synagogues, and had designed a number of important synagogues nationwide by the early 1950s. While he was responsible for the overall design of the complex, Albert Kahn Associates completed the working drawings and all engineering for the project.

The members of Congregation Shaarey Zedek approved the purchase of the land for the synagogue in the Detroit suburb of Southfield in 1957. The cornerstone was laid in early 1962, and the congregation held its first services in October of that year. A formal dedication was held in January 1963.

Shaarey Zedek comprises three buildings: the synagogue, a school, and a community or social center. Contained within these interconnected buildings are the fifteen thousand-square-foot sanctuary, two smaller chapels, a library, a garden court, and administrative offices. The sanctuary can be expanded to accommodate between twelve hundred and thirty-five hundred worshippers.

The sanctuary is diamond-shaped in plan and constructed of reinforced concrete. Its soaring southern wall is reminiscent of a tent and rises ninety feet into the air. A band of recessed stained-glass windows separates the metal roof from the concrete walls, and gives the impression that the roof is floating above the structure. Triangular windows, set in cast concrete, admit daylight into the sanctuary on the east and west elevations.

For the interior, Goodman turned to his wife, interior designer Naomi Ascher, whom he married in 1944. While Goodman designed some of the furniture for Shaarey Zedek, Ms. Asher, doing business as Goodman Interiors, Ltd., provided the interior design. In fact, she worked on the interior design for many of Goodman's other synagogues.

The stained-glass panels in the sanctuary were created by noted stained glass artist Robert Pinart, and produced by Cummings Stained Glass Studio of Massachusetts. Pinart, born in Paris, France, and educated at the Ecole des Beaux Arts, emigrated to the United States in 1951. His designs have been installed in numerous buildings throughout the country, including the National Cathedral in Washington, DC.

Landscape design was provided by Eichstedt, Grissim, Young & Associates, a landscape architecture and site planning firm in Grosse Pointe, Michigan.

Percival Goodman was born in New York City on January 13, 1904. After receiving his architectural training at the Ecole des Beaux-Arts in Paris from 1925 to 1929, he established his own firm in New York City in 1936 and designed a wide range of building types. In 1939, his entry for the Smithsonian Gallery of Art competition placed second to that of Eliel Saarinen, Eero Saarinen, and J. Robert F. Swanson.

During the 1940s, Goodman designed individual apartments and apartment buildings, single family residences, department stores, industrial plants, educational buildings, and furniture, and produced numerous reports and plans for improving various facets of New York City. It was not until 1948 that Goodman designed his first synagogues–five in that year alone–but he quickly established his reputation as a designer of first-rate religious buildings. In the decades that followed, he designed some fifty ecclesiastical buildings, chiefly synagogues, across the country.

Besides practicing as an architect, Goodman was equally influential as an educator, theorist, critic, and author. He taught at Columbia University School of Architecture from 1946 to 1971. In 1947 he published Communitas, which he wrote with his brother Paul Goodman, the noted writer, philosopher, and sociologist. In Communitas the Goodmans assessed the condition of planning and the built environment in American at mid-century. Percival Goodman later wrote The Double E, which applied ecological principles to city planning.

The synagogue complex of Congregation Shaarey Zedek preserves virtually all of Goodman's original design. An addition was made to the north end of the school wing and youth lounge in 1964, and the original terne metal roof was replaced with galvanized sheet metal in 1990.

ST. FRANCIS DE SALES CHURCH

MARCEL BREUER, 1964-66

NORTON SHORES.

St. Francis de Sales Catholic Parish was founded in Norton Shores in 1948 and built its first church two years later across the street from this remarkable church building. By 1958, the parish had outgrown its original sanctuary, and plans for construction of a new one were initiated. Father Louis LePres, the church pastor since 1955, spearheaded the project that awarded Marcel Breuer the commission to design the new church in 1961. The design process took several years, and construction began in 1964 and was completed in 1966.

St. Francis de Sales Church soars above its residential neighborhood with a monumental seventy-five-foot-high, banner-like, trapezoidal front façade that seems to reach out to embrace all. The hyperbolic paraboloid side walls of poured concrete make the building seem to be in constant motion, appearing to thrust out the front façade proudly. The front façade is topped with a concrete trough that houses the three large church bells protruding over the front wall.

Twelve angular concrete arches span the interior space connecting the trapezoidal front and rear walls. The interior plan of the nave narrows from front to back to focus on the altar, and is connected to a rectangular chapter house behind the nave. The legs of the arches are expressed behind the altar as columns representing the twelve apostles. The double curvature of the side walls tends to distort perspective, yet the interior is symmetrical with the central altar at the front and a full-width balcony suspended at the rear. The perspective distortion creates a sense of movement as one walks around the interior. The entrance to the sanctuary is located under the balcony creating an awe-inspiring entrance from the compressed height under the balcony to the soaring height of the main sanctuary. The ratio of the nave's height to width makes the priest appear to be much closer to the worshipers than in actuality.

Marcel Breuer was born in Hungary in 1883 and studied under Walter Gropius, Mies van der Rohe, and Le Corbusier at the Bauhaus in Germany. When Breuer left Germany in 1935 to join Walter Gropius in London, he had become one of the leading designers in Europe. In 1937, he emigrated to the United States at the invitation of Joseph Hudnut, University of Michigan graduate and dean of the Graduate School of Design at Harvard, to join Gropius on the faculty. He moved to New York City in 1946 to establish his own architectural practice. Breuer's commissions and reputation grew steadily. When he received the commission to design St. Francis de Sales, he had just completed St. John's Abbey in Collegeville, Minnesota, and his commission for the Whitney Museum in New York City was well underway.

Breuer collaborated with his design associate Herbert Beckhard on St. Francis de Sales Church as well as other projects. The two architects received a Silver Medal from the American Institute of Architects for the design of St. Francis de Sales Church. The jury said of the church, "The inner space conveys a powerful religious experience, the whole concept had great dignity."

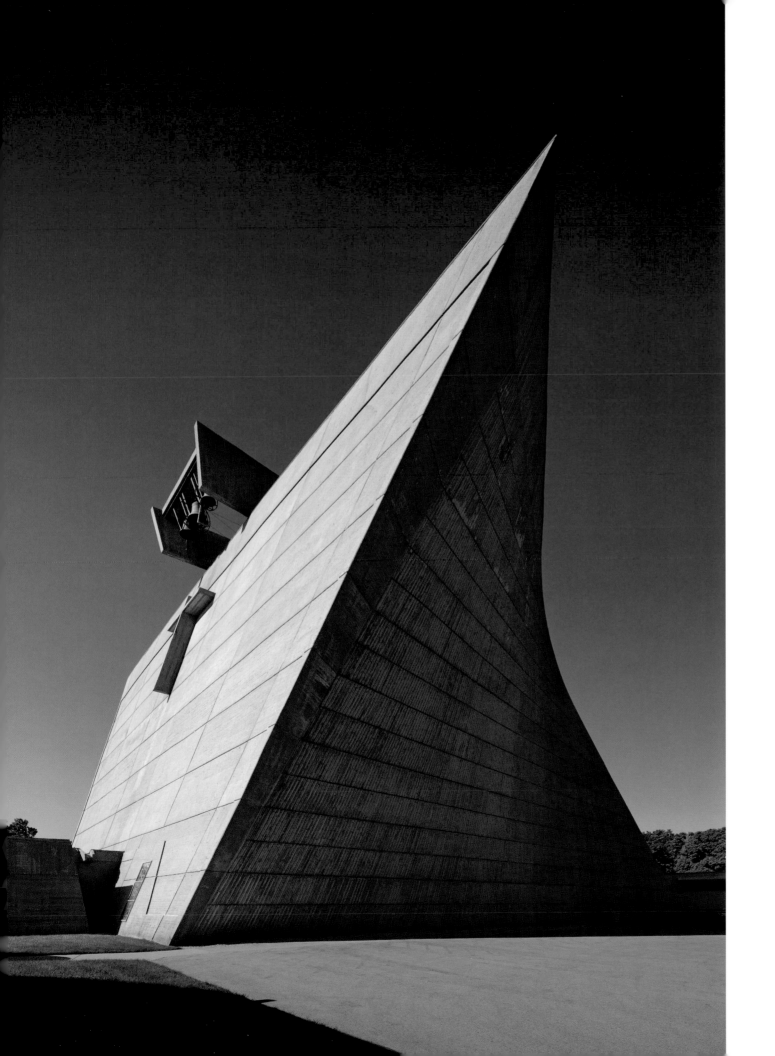

Perspective is visually distorted by the double curvature of the side walls.

The white domed Schwartz House sits like an igloo in a lush green clearing in the woods adjacent to Sturgeon Creek in Midland. Deceptively small in appearance, it is a three-story, thin shell, hemispherical dome structure with a circular plan. The dome structure consists of layers of two-by-four-by-ten-inch extruded polystyrene boards stacked and heat fused using the Spiral Generation method of construction developed and patented by the Midland-based Dow Chemical Company. The polystyrene dome structure is covered with a three-inch-thick coating of concrete sprayed over a grid of reinforcing steel. Three fifteen-foot-tall arched openings are cut from the dome and infilled with aluminum-framed window walls.

During World War II, researchers at Dow Chemical found a way to foam polystyrene and later developed methods to extrude it as a lightweight, closed-cell material that resists moisture and offers high insulation qualities. It was patented and trademarked by Dow Chemical with the brand name Styrofoam in 1944. Looking for new ways to utilize Styrofoam, a Dow Chemical research and development engineer, Donald R. Wright, developed a technique and a machine to form strips of Styrofoam to build dome structures. It was patented as Spiral Generation and introduced in 1963. The Spiral Generation machine used to create the dome consisted of a steel boom anchored at the center of the circular plan. A heat-welding device that bent, laid, and sealed together the Styrofoam boards rotated around the center pivot-point, adding layer upon layer of Styrofoam board in a spiral gradually decreasing in circumference to form the dome. Dow Chemical Company erected a forty-five foot diameter prototype case study dome to serve as a temporary clubhouse for a golf course just outside of Ann Arbor. The case study dome was erected in June 1963 and took only about twelve hours to complete. The construction technique allowed for rapid construction without the need for scaffolding or interior supports. By 1965 Dow's Spiral Generation technique had been used to construct waste water treatment equipment shelters in Midland, a domed theater and convention addition to the Park Place Hotel in Traverse City, Michigan, a planetarium at the University of Toledo, a clinic in Lafayette, Indiana, and classrooms for the Roper School in Detroit. However, it was never adopted as a popular construction technique.

Robert Schwartz, a Midland native, graduated from the University of Michigan's College of Architecture and Design in 1954. In his senior year at the university, Schwartz participated in a special project led by R. Buckminster Fuller, an architect, inventor and author best known as the inventor of the Geodesic Dome. Fuller was a guest lecturer at the university who visited the architecture program often while working on his geodesic dome for the Ford Motor Company in nearby Dearborn. The special class project was to design and construct a dome shelter using cardboard to house young boys in programs at Camp Tamarack, a camping and recreational facility managed by the Jewish Community Center of Detroit. Fuller, with the assistance of University of Michigan faculty members George Brigham and Walter Sanders, led students in the design and construction of the cardboard dome structure. The project's specific requirements stipulated that it be lightweight, easily erected and disassembled, low cost, and able to accommodate six boys. Schwartz was named the project's graphics director. The project took place in just over a week and culminated in the construction of a prototype shelter on the grounds of Alpha Chi Rho fraternity in Ann Arbor.

By the early 1960s, Schwartz and his wife Barbara had three children, and Schwartz had partnered with Charles Blacklock to form the architectural firm of Blacklock & Schwartz. Recalling his involvement with Fuller and the student dome project, and his knowledge of Dow Chemical's experiments with Styrofoam dome construction, Schwartz began to think about incorporating a dome in a home for his family. In 1964, Schwartz entered into an agreement with Dow Chemical Company to use the Spiral Generation method in constructing his house. Dow would supply the equipment and materials to construct the dome in return for studying and monitoring the construction as a prototype for residential construction. The construction of the Styrofoam dome took only about fourteen hours to complete, with the application of an outer coating of reinforcing steel and concrete taking several additional weeks. With the interior completed, the family moved in 1966.

The three-floor interior of the house is surprisingly spacious. The hexagonal-shaped second and third floors do not intersect the dome, but instead float on columns within the dome's larger volume. The open plan and large walls of windows in three directions provide natural light and expansive views of the surrounding landscape. Given that the Spiral Generation machine could not complete the top of the dome, a five-foot diameter skylight caps the volume and brings light into the upper level. There are four bedrooms on the second level and a wide-open space on the third level, encircled by the curve of the dome with the hexagonal floor held away from the dome's surface. A graceful central circular staircase connects all three levels.

In partnership with Blacklock, Robert E. Schwartz designed several commercial, institutional, and government buildings in the Midland area, including the United Church of Christ (1961) with its dramatic thin-shell hyperbolic paraboloid roof structure, before dissolving the partnership in 1974. He is credited with designing between twenty and thirty single-family residences in Midland before his death in 2010, though no others were built utilizing the Styrofoam Spiral Generation technique.

ROBERT AND BARBARA
SCHWARTZ HOUSE

ROBERT E. SCHWARTZ, 1964-66

MIDLAND.

Above, Dining room separated from living room by decorative screen.
Right, Central spiral staircase connecting three levels.

W. HAWKINS FERRY HOUSE

WILLIAM KESSLER, 1964

GROSSE POINTE SHORES.

The W. Hawkins Ferry House was constructed in 1964 on a site in Grosse Pointe Shores with mature pines and maples and a sweeping view of Lake St. Clair. W. Hawkins Ferry commissioned architect William H. Kessler to design a house for his family that Ferry envisioned as a synthesis of architecture, art, and landscape architecture.

W. Hawkins Ferry was born in 1913 to Dexter M. Ferry Jr. and Jeannette Hawkins Ferry. Dexter Ferry was the son of one of the founders of the Ferry-Morse Seed Company in Detroit, at one time the largest seed company in the world. His son was educated at Cranbrook School for Boys in Bloomfield Hills, and later studied architecture under Walter Gropius and Marcel Breuer at Harvard University.

Upon graduating from Harvard, Ferry returned to Detroit and almost immediately began what became a lifetime of collecting, advocating, and supporting the arts and architecture. He amassed a personal art collection of twentieth century works of such scope that it included surrealist and abstract expressionist pieces. In 1946, he began to assist the Detroit Institute of Art (DIA) in purchasing significant works of modern art. That year, DIA director William Valentiner and Ferry arranged an exhibition, Origins of Modern Sculpture, which featured works by Detroit artists and sculptors such as Carl Milles, Marshall Fredericks, Samuel Cashwan, and Alexander Girard, set in context with historic and prehistoric sculpture. Eventually, Ferry's support of the DIA led to him to serve as a trustee of the museum's Founders Society, president of the Friends of Modern Art, advisor to the City of Detroit Arts Commission, honorary curator for the DIA, and chairman of the Metropolitan Art Association. By 1966, he had provided the DIA with eighteen of its most important modern pieces, and was considered one of this country's greatest experts on modern and contemporary art. His patronage and personal collections led to an exhibition held at the DIA in 1966, The W. Hawkins Ferry Collection. A second exhibition of thirty-eight works from Ferry's personal collection was mounted in 1987.

Ferry's interest in art and his work with the DIA were complemented by his interest in architecture. In the early 1940s, Ferry organized a DIA exhibition, A Cross Section of Detroit Architecture, 1823-1943, that documented the city's architectural past. He subsequently wrote The Buildings of Detroit: A History, a comprehensive look at Detroit's architectural history, in 1968, and authored a second book, The Legacy of Albert Kahn, documenting Kahn's architectural achievements, two years later.

Through his extensive connections, Ferry brought many prominent architects to Detroit for lectures, for which he received an honorary membership in the Michigan Society of Architects in 1954. In 1969, he was appointed by Governor William G. Milliken to a committee to review designs for a new capitol building. Though the building was never constructed, Ferry participated in design reviews alongside some of Michigan's most significant architects and designers of the 1960s and 1970s, including Glen Paulsen, Walter B. Sanders, Pipsan Saarinen Swanson, Gino Rossetti, William Kessler, Sol King, and Alden B. Dow.

For many years, Ferry had dreamed of a house that would be the ultimate in modern architecture to showcase his art collection. Foremost in his mind was a two-story living room with a dramatic staircase and one wall consisting only of glass. Kessler designed a home that exceeded Ferry's vision.

The house is designed on a fifteen-by-fifteen-foot grid, with each façade consisting of four bays. The west façade contains the main entrance, a grand door set in a wall of glass. The east façade, facing the lake, is entirely glass set in metal frames. The house is sheltered by its flat roof's wide overhang. A band of windows where the exterior walls meet the roof makes the roof seem to float above the walls. Within its planning grid, the interior comprises an array of varying cubic volumes that flow from west to east, proceeding from the entry toward the lake with volumes expanding and compressing. The two-story entrance volume leads to a one-story space containing a custom-designed circular staircase of pre-cast terrazzo slabs lit from above by a pattern of circular skylights. The cubic volumes, neutral colors, and natural materials provided ideal exhibition space for Ferry's art collection.

William Kessler received a bachelor's degree in architecture in 1948 from the Chicago Institute of Design, which merged with the Illinois Institute of Technology in 1949. He then enrolled in Harvard University Graduate School of Design, studying under Walter Gropius. After graduation in 1950, Kessler remained at Harvard as an instructor of design, but left in 1951 to join Leinweber, Yamasaki & Hellmuth in Detroit. Kessler and colleague Philip Meathe left Yamasaki & Leinweber in 1955 to establish Meathe, Kessler and Associates in Grosse Pointe, Michigan. Over the following eighteen years, the firm produced many significant and award-winning works that ranged from residences to educational and commercial buildings.

When Meathe joined Smith, Hinchman & Grylls in 1969, Kessler reorganized the firm as William Kessler and Associates. The firm completed numerous college buildings as well as such important commissions as Detroit Receiving Hospital and Michigan Library and Historical Center, in Lansing. In 1999, Kessler established Kessler Francis Cardoza Architects with Ed Francis and Jim Cardoza. The firm merged with Gunn Levine Architects in 2004, two years after Kessler's death, and was reorganized as Resendes Design Group in 2010.

The Ferry House was widely acknowledged in the media. Architectural Record named the Ferry House a Record House in 1965, House Beautiful featured it in its September 1969 edition, and architecture critics of the Detroit Free Press and the Detroit News both praised the design in extensive essays. Kessler received numerous awards and honors throughout his long career, including the American Institute of Architects Gold Medal in 1974 and 1976, the Hastings Award in 1984, and the Charles A. Blessing Award in 1996.

Floating circular staircase at front entry with skylight above.

Left, Front entry.
Right, Balcony overlooking
two story living room.

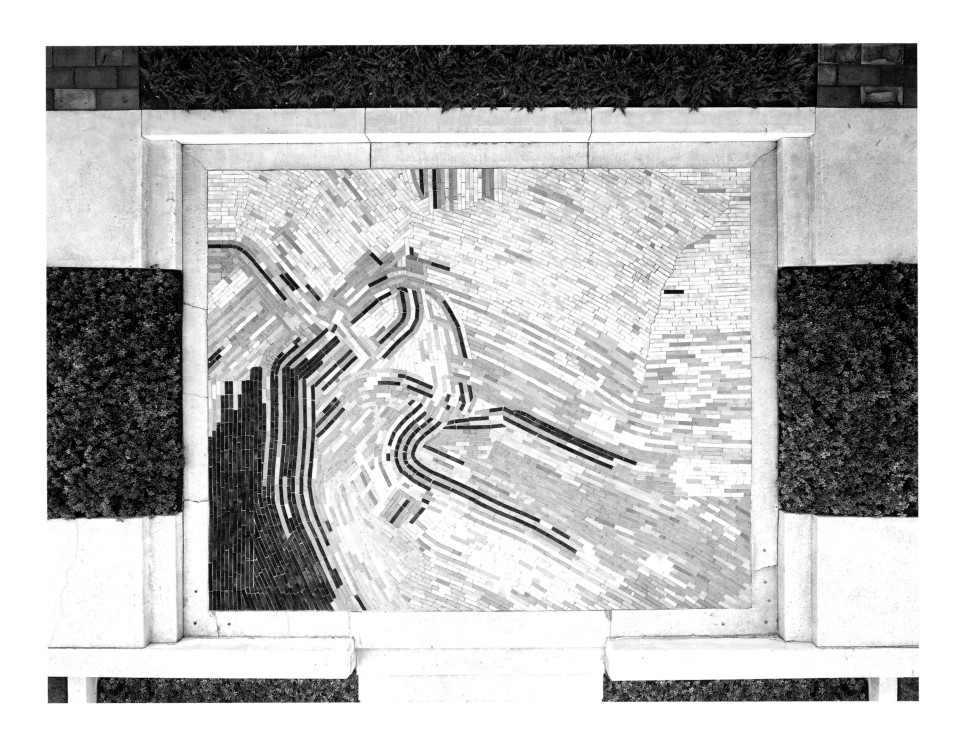

Above, Decorative tile mosaic on patio designed by Glen Michaels.

DONALD AND HARRIET FREEMAN HOUSE

GUNNAR BIRKERTS, 1965-66

EAST
GRAND
RAPIDS.

Nestled in a heavily-wooded lot in East Grand Rapids, the Freeman House stands out against the classically styled neighboring houses as, in the words of Harriet Freeman, a "modern adaptation of an ancient Greek island house."

Inspired by a trip to Greece, Harriet Freeman wrote to Gunnar Birkerts in April 1964 to gauge his interest in designing a house for her family. In her letter, she laid out her vision for what they sought—a house that was sculptural, yet simple, designed to exude a "casual formality" and serve as "refuge from the racing pace . . . and resultant tensions" of modern life. Her desired black-and-white interior would serve as a background for color, books, furniture, and "an active participation in music and art." In physical terms, the Freemans' intentions for the house included a central atrium—an enchanted inner court—that would provide visual delight and "a breathing space—a release from other confinements."

In the rest of the letter, Harriet Freeman discussed specific requirements for each section of the house: a comfortable living room, a light-filled kitchen, and a service area closed off from the rest of house to discourage "all those meter-reading men who love to catch one in a nightgown!" Birkerts replied just a few weeks later, saying he was "fascinated with the opportunity" to design the house. Writing to the Freemans again in July 1964, he informed them that he was beginning to design their "fascinating house." Preliminary drawings were sent to the Freemans in February 1965, and, after minor alterations, construction began. The house was completed in 1966.

Contemplating the Freeman House years later, Birkerts recalled that his clients' requests caused him to "search for new principles" that would allow him to create the "unrestrained" building the couple envisioned. At first, Birkerts admitted, self-imposed constraints prevented him from visualizing such a structure, but by superimposing an orthogonal planning grid over a radial grid, he realized his solution. The answer, he intuited, was an eccentric center atrium with surrounding spaces set at irregular degrees. Thus, every interior wall, extending from the atrium to an exterior wall, is angled toward and provides views of the atrium, creating unfolding vistas as one moves about the house. Windows along the exterior walls provide light and views.

Gunnar Birkerts was born in Riga, Latvia, in 1925. He attended the Technische Hochschule in Stuttgart, Germany, where he earned degrees in architecture and engineering, and became aware of the work of Eliel and Eero Saarinen. After graduating in 1949, he left Stuttgart for Michigan to work for the Saarinens. Upon arriving in Bloomfield Hills, Birkerts walked up to Eero Saarinen's house unannounced to ask for a job. Having no position available but impressed by Birkerts nonetheless, Saarinen referred him to the Chicago firm of Perkins and Will. By 1951, Saarinen was engaged in the design of the General Motors Technical Center, in Warren, and invited Birkerts to join his firm. Between 1951 and 1955, Birkerts worked as a designer on the Center and the Milwaukee War Memorial Building. Birkerts left Eero Saarinen and Associates in 1955 and worked for a short time in Milwaukee, Wisconsin, with Donald Grieb. At the invitation of Minoru Yamasaki, Birkerts left Grieb's office in 1956, and returned to Michigan to spend the next three years at Yamasaki, Leinweber and Associates, where he served as the chief designer for several significant projects. He was made partner in 1959, but decided shortly thereafter that it was his "turn to speak."

Birkerts left Yamasaki's office with Frank Straub to establish Birkerts and Straub in 1959. When the partnership ended in 1963, Birkerts founded the firm of Gunnar Birkerts and Associates. It was also about this time that Birkerts began teaching at the University of Michigan's College of Architecture and design. He was appointed an assistant professor of architecture in 1961, and became a professor of architecture in 1969. Upon retiring from academia in 1990, Birkerts was named a professor emeritus by the university, and received a Distinguished Professor Award from the Association of Collegiate Schools of Architecture. He was practicing architecture in Wellesley, Massachusetts, where he moved to be closer to family, at the time of his death in 2017.

Birkerts completed a remarkable portfolio of work, including Domino Farms, in Ann Arbor; the Contemporary Arts Museum, in Houston, Texas; the Federal Reserve Bank of Minneapolis; the Corning Glass Museum, in Corning, New York; and most recently the National Library of Latvia, in Riga, Latvia. He received numerous architectural awards, including three Progressive Architecture Design Award Citations (1957, 1959, and 1960); American Institute of Architects College of Fellows (1970); American Institute of Architects, Detroit Gold Medal (1975); American Academy in Rome, Architect in Residence (1976); Michigan Society of Architects Gold Medal (1980); Arnold W. Brunner Memorial Prize in Architecture, American Academy of the Institute of Arts and Letters (1981); the Order of Three Stars from the Republic of Latvia (1995); and an American Institute of Architect Building Award for the National Library of Latvia (2017). Birkerts was awarded the 1968 Architectural Record Award of Excellence for his design of the Freeman House.

Study area lit by projecting bays.

Left, Rear patio area,
Above, Master bedroom.

UNITED AUTO WORKERS FAMILY EDUCATION CENTER

OSKAR STONOROV, 1967-70

ONAWAY

Walter Reuther joined the Ford Motor Company as a tool and die maker in 1927, but soon dedicated his life to organizing auto laborers. He was instrumental in the establishment of the United Auto Workers (UAW) in 1935. It was Reuther's role in the Flint Sit-Down Strike of 1937 that made him a rising star in the fledgling union, and he was elected UAW president in 1946. As the UAW's leader, he focused on its Education Department, which had been part of the union since its inception. Initially, the UAW purchased a former National Youth Administration Camp, renamed Camp FDR, near Port Huron, Michigan, where it operated "Weekend Institutes" that taught over 35,000 laborers. (The Students for a Democratic Society wrote its Manifesto for the New Left at Camp FDR in 1962.) Reuther had long been displeased with the camp's poor physical condition and state of disrepair. Having vowed to build a series of new labor education centers around the country, he obtained UAW funding in 1966 for a new center to be located in northern Michigan.

After scouting a number of sites, the UAW purchased the former summer home of Detroit sports advertising pioneer Louis R. Maxon in 1967. Located on Black Lake near the city of Onaway, Michigan, the one thousand-acre site still retains many of the buildings associated with Maxon, including a 1932 timber lodge where Lucille Ball and Desi Arnaz spent their honeymoon. The UAW Family Education Center, now known as the Black Lake Conference Center, is a striking blend of these historic buildings and modern buildings designed by architect Oscar Stonorov.

Reuther originally conceived of the new education center as a place to develop "tomorrow's leaders." The center was intended to uplift the spirit and offer a place of rest and renewal for urban workers and their families, educating the next generation of autoworkers about the early struggles for unionization. Workers would acquire the knowledge to help them embark on their own leadership paths, and receive a wide range of information to help improve the condition of their daily lives. The development of the education center was Reuther's dream project and no expense was spared. Stonorov, best known for his innovative public housing work in Philadelphia, served as chief designer. But Reuther was deeply involved in the complex's design and development, and it became a labor of love for him as his career neared its end. An early environmentalist, Reuther worked closely with Stonorov to ensure that the complex preserved the site's original landscape. Trees were left untouched and the utility system was placed underground in order to retain as much of the site's natural beauty as possible.

Constructed between 1967 and 1970, Stonorov's buildings occupy the center of the complex. Overlooking a broad section of Fisher Creek, the main conference center consists of a hotel, classroom building, Olympic-size indoor swimming pool, gymnasium with two full-size basketball courts, four hundred-seat dining room, and twelve hundred-seat lecture hall, all connected by covered, glass-enclosed walkways. There is a wealth of thoughtful details. A meditation room features a sculpture of the zodiac as it appeared on the day of Reuther's birth, a gift from the construction trade union that built the center. The red cedar siding and local Onaway stone used on the exterior give warmth to the modern design, while massive windows bring the outdoors in. (Tennessee Crab Orchard stone was substituted after the Onaway quarry closed.) The decorative bronze metal and stone pieces found throughout the complex were imported from Italy. Wood is deployed for its strength and beauty, including laminated beams up to forty feet long and sixteen inches in diameter, massive columns turned in the state of Washington by a maker of ship masts, and roofs built to withstand up to five feet of snowfall.

Unfortunately, Walter Reuther and Oskar Stonorov did not live to see the project completed. In 1970 they died together in a plane crash on their way to visit the site. Reuther's ashes were spread in the arboretum that overlooks the Black Lake Conference Center.

*Left, Fireplace in main lobby with metal
sculpture donated by Italian union members.*

*Above, Circular meditation room
with signs of Zodiac sculpture.
Right, Dining hall.*

Above, Outside the gymnasium.
Right, Hallways connecting buildings.

CHURCH OF ST. MARY

WILLIAM WESLEY PETERS, 1969

ALMA.

The Church of St. Mary's dramatically sweeping concave conical roofs and spires rest on curved concrete block walls, contrasting with the modest buildings in the surrounding neighborhood just north of the main commercial corridor of Alma. Everywhere one looks, the exterior offers fascinating details. The central conical roof spire contains a swirling stained-glass window that winds dramatically up the spire. The main entrance is protected beneath a graceful concrete rounded and arched canopy that reaches out to invite worshipers in. The canopy is reflected in wide, curved concrete steps leading up to the doors. The concrete block walls are set with overlapping edges, creating a textured or patterned appearance to the walls.

Not surprisingly, the interior is equally memorable. The plan is a series of intersecting circles with a rectilinear L-shaped wing extending from the rear and housing the rectory. The sanctuary stands beneath the large conical dome and spire, with exposed curved interior beams rising to the center. Its carpet-covered pews with seating for approximately seven hundred worshipers are set in gently curved rows rising from the altar area on a sloped floor. The smaller conical dome circular area houses a small sanctuary.

William Wesley Peters, the architect of the Church of St. Mary, was one of Frank Lloyd Wright's first apprentices when Wright founded the Taliesin Fellowship in Spring Green, Wisconsin in 1932. Peters remained at Wright's side for over two decades, serving as structural engineer and project architect on many Wright projects, including the Guggenheim Museum, in New York, the Johnson Wax Administration Building, in Racine, Wisconsin, and Fallingwater, in Mill Run, Pennsylvania. In 1935, he married Wright's adopted daughter, Svetlana, who died in an automobile accident in 1946. He was later briefly married to the daughter of Joseph Stalin, Svetlana Alliluyeva.

Following Wright's death in 1959, Peters became chairman of Taliesin Associated Architects. He designed a variety of structures throughout the country that incorporate the organic influence of Wright and the Taliesin Fellowship. The Church of St. Mary continues the exploration of the circular plans Wright used in the latter years of his career. The result is a futuristic looking building that is a landmark in Alma.

Main sanctuary under the main conical dome.

*Small chapel under the
secondary conical dome.*

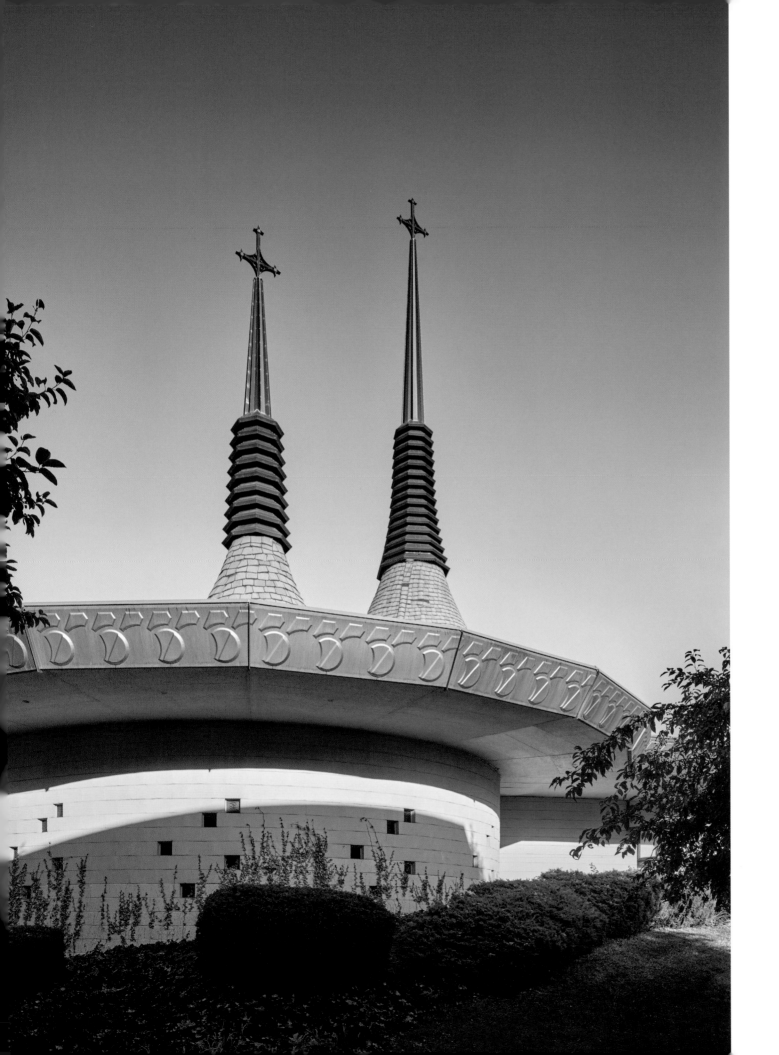

POWER CENTER FOR THE PERFORMING ARTS

KEVIN ROCHE, 1970-71

ANN ARBOR.

In 1963, Eugene and Sadye Power, longtime supporters of the theater program at the University of Michigan, joined with their son Philip in making a $3 million donation to the school for the construction of a new performing arts facility. The Power Center for the Performing Arts was conceived to satisfy the need for a proscenium-stage theater on campus. It fills a gap between the massive but technically limited Hill Auditorium, designed by Albert Kahn, and the much smaller Lydia Mendelssohn Theater.

The Power Center was designed by Kevin Roche John Dinkeloo and Associates, with architect Kevin Roche as principal designer and architect/engineer John Dinkeloo handling the engineering and technical aspects. Sited on the eastern edge of Fitch Park, the last remaining open space on the central campus, the theater combines massive concrete columns and walls with mirrored glass to reflect the mature trees on the lawn in front. The eight-foot-diameter hollow concrete columns carry large steel box beams that span 145 feet from the front to the concrete-walled stage house. The glass becomes clear when backlit at night so the building comes alive with the activity and excitement of theater patrons. The spacious and soaring grand lobby running the full width of the building boasts two sculptural concrete circular staircases with bridges leading to balcony seating. The theater's interior was created by set designer Jo Mielziner, and echoes his work in the Vivian Beaumont Theater at Lincoln Center in New York, with a stage representing an experimental combination of proscenium and thrust configurations, and seating that is no more than eighty feet from the stage. Open in 1971, the Center achieves a seemingly contradictory combination of soaring interior space and an intimate theater setting.

Eamonn Kevin Roche was born in Ireland in 1922. After graduating from University College in Dublin in 1945, he left Ireland in the following year to study under Ludwig Mies van der Rohe at the Illinois Institute of Technology. He joined the firm of Eero Saarinen and Associates in Bloomfield Hills in 1950, and became principal design associate in 1954.

Kevin Roche John Dinkeloo and Associates is a direct outgrowth of Eero Saarinen and Associates. Roche and Dinkeloo were partners in Saarinen's firm in Bloomfield Hills, and oversaw the completion of the firm's commissions following Saarinen's sudden death in 1961. Upon the completion of the Saarinen projects and the closing of the Bloomfield Hills office, they formed Kevin Roche John Dinkeloo and Associates in 1966 in Hamden, Connecticut. The firm has completed the designs and master plans for over two hundred built projects in the United States and internationally. Roche received the prestigious Pritzker Prize for Architecture in 1982 and was awarded an American Institute of Architects Gold Medal in 1993. Since Dinkeloo's death in 1981, Kevin Roche and Christiaan Dinkeloo have led the firm's team of partners, associates and directors.

One of a pair of sculptural spiral staircases
with bridges leading to balcony seating.

219

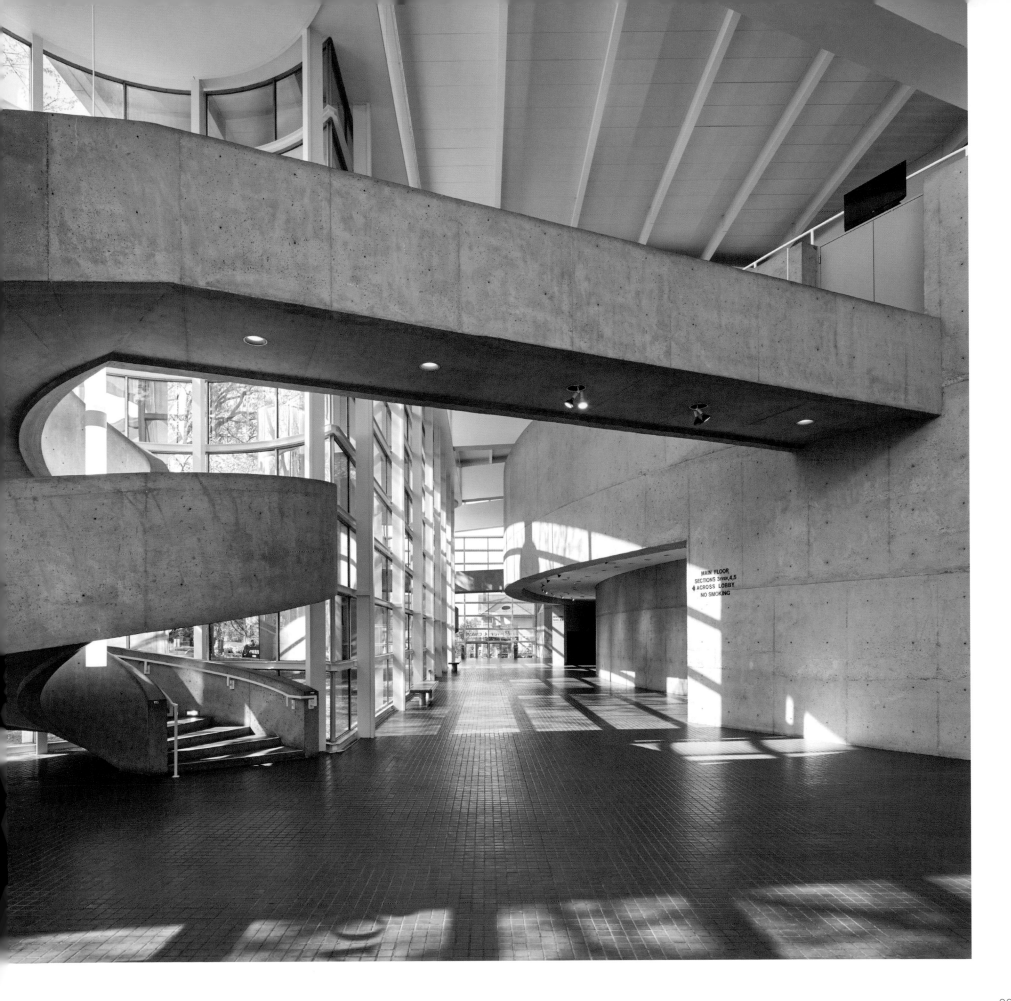

MAIN FLOOR
SECTIONS 3MEZZ, 4, 5
◄ACROSS LOBBY
NO SMOKING

JAMES AND JEAN
DOUGLAS HOUSE

RICHARD MEIER, 1971-73

HARBOR
SPRINGS.

James and Jean Douglas and their three children planned to transition to a slower pace of life in the beautiful area north of Harbor Springs. They contacted architect Richard Meier about designing a house after seeing pictures of Meier's Smith House (1967), in Darien, Connecticut. Jim Douglas managed a trucking company in Grand Rapids established by his father. The Douglases were drawn to the clean lines and modern design of the Smith House, and wanted to duplicate it as a northern Michigan residence.

The Douglases had originally planned to build the house in the community of L'Arbe Croche on Little Traverse Bay, just south of Harbor Springs. That gated community had strict rules for home design and landscaping, reinforcing a natural environment with earth-toned exteriors, minimal tree removal and naturalized landscaping. That was all well and good with the Douglases. However, the white exterior of a Meier house was rejected by L'Arbe Croche. Since Meier's design had to be white, they found another lot. The rejection from L'Arbe Croche made all the difference, because the couple found a steeply sloped lot on Lake Michigan in Friendship Township, north of Harbor Springs, which added to the significance and striking views of the completed house. Meier modified his design to accommodate the site, with the entry at the top level and the house dropping three floors below on the steep hillside. The result was a dramatic white architectural statement that seems to be hanging on the hillside above the shoreline, nestled in the greenery of cedar and conifer trees.

The overall form of the house is a rectangular box set on end into the side of the steeply sloped hillside, resting on a foundation of telephone pole-like pilings that create a level platform. The exterior walls are flush tongue-and-groove vertical redwood, painted white, forming a vertical mass that is open to the view of the lake through a geometrically articulated large window wall. A projecting, curving metal exterior staircase and two cylindrical metal ship-like smoke stacks contrast with the rectangular geometry, adding interest to the lake-facing façade. The house brilliantly exploits its topography. As one approaches from the street-level parking area by a bridge to the fourth-level entry, what appears to be a one-story structure descends to reveal four distinct levels. The main living spaces rise through multiple levels. The entrance to the house provides a breathtaking view of living areas below while providing an experience of soaring over Lake Michigan with unobstructed views beyond the expansive glass wall. In signature Meier style, all interior and exterior wall surfaces are simple, unornamented and painted white.

Space flows virtually unimpeded inside. The upper entry level looks down over the two-story-high living room on level two. This upper level also opens to a full width roof deck overlooking the lake. The third level contains three of the five bedrooms and a guest bathroom. The first level contains the kitchen and dining rooms with openings to the floor above. Two additional bedrooms are stacked on the first and second levels. The interior treatment reflects Meier's penchant for simplicity, minimalism and streamlined modern design. Original furnishings include pieces by Le Corbusier, Mies van der Rohe, Alvar Aalto and Richard Meier.

Meier has achieved global recognition for his architecture. The Douglas House, his only work in Michigan, is perhaps one of his most recognized residential works. It has been featured in numerous architectural publications and was named as one of America's favorite architectural structures, one of just twelve homes in a list of 150 structures, by the American Institute of Architects in 2007.

After receiving a degree in architecture from Cornell University in 1957, Meier gained early professional experience working in New York for Skidmore, Owings and Merrill and for Marcel Breuer, a highly esteemed Bauhaus instructor and exponent of Modernism. Meier established his own practice in New York in 1963. The success of the first residences he designed helped launch his career. For example, critical acclaim for the Smith House, in Darien, Connecticut, caught the attention of the Douglases. The Smith House and the Douglas House were Meier's first commissions to reflect the Modernist spirit of Le Corbusier's work of the 1920s and 1930s. Building on the success and publicity surrounding the Douglas House, he began to receive large public commissions, including the Getty Center, in Los Angeles, completed in 1997, and has subsequently focused his career on larger commercial and institutional projects of note. Meier has received numerous awards for his work, including the prestigious Pritzker Architecture Award in 1984.

A meticulous restoration of the house was completed by the third owners in 2016 with guidance from Richard Meier Associates.

Page 228,
Bridge from parking
area to main entrance.
Right, Suspended metal
staircase connecting
balcony levels.

Rooftop deck at sunset.

MINORU AND TERUKO YAMASAKI HOUSE

MINORU YAMASAKI, 1972

BLOOMFIELD
TOWNSHIP.

Minoru Yamasaki built this residence for his family in Bloomfield Township, outside Detroit, at the peak of his career in 1972. Noted chiefly for his commercial and institutional buildings, Yamasaki designed approximately twenty-one residences in Michigan between 1950 and 1954 before concentrating on larger commissions. The design for his own house nearly two decades later reflects an elegantly simplified evolution from his earlier residential work, incorporating simplified geometric forms, open floor plans, structural clarity, integration into the site's natural landscaping, and a lack of the ornamentation that adorned his larger buildings. The house is a two-story, flat-roofed structure with an L-shaped plan and a one-story front elevation. Drawing inspiration from Japanese architecture, Yamasaki brought order and tranquility to his seven-thousand-square-foot residence. Noting that a Japanese interior is meant to be a background for people, elegant and beautiful in its simplicity, he designed the interior to recede quietly, allowing the furniture, artwork and people to become the focal point of each room. Applying this philosophy to his own work, he endeavored to create buildings that would serve as thoughtful and tranquil backgrounds for activities rather than spectacles meant to awe and impress. Thus, the Yamasaki House is an understated structure with large spaces.

When Minoru and Teruko Yamasaki arrived in Detroit in 1945, they found it difficult to find suitable housing for their growing family. Despite the fact that Yamasaki was a successful architect and the couple exemplified well-educated American citizens, they were stymied in their search by persistent anti-Japanese sentiment. The Yamasakis eventually purchased a somewhat rundown farmhouse in Troy, some twenty miles north of Detroit. By the early 1970s the area had developed with commercial buildings; they were able to sell the property at a handsome price and begin thinking about designing and building a new home. After twenty-five years, they purchased land and constructed a house in a community that previously excluded them. The house features an open floor plan, minimal ornamentation, and large expanses of glass for natural light, all reflecting Yamasaki's desire to create a living space that imparts a sense of peace and serenity.

Minoru Yamasaki was born in Seattle, Washington in 1912, the son of Japanese immigrants. Yamasaki's first introduction to architecture occurred in 1926 during his sophomore year in high school. A visit from an uncle who had just graduated from architecture school in California and brought some of his drawings with him was transformative for the young man. Yamasaki began his formal architectural education at the University of Washington, and moved to New York after graduation. Finding few job opportunities in the city due to the Great Depression, Yamasaki enrolled in graduate school at New York University, where he also taught a course in painting. He then worked for several New York architectural firms, including collaboration between George Nelson and Raymond Loewy.

Before long, Yamasaki's career would take him to Michigan. From the 1930s through the post-World War II era, Michigan attracted many young talented architects and designers. They found an atmosphere of atmosphere of creativity and innovation driven by the automobile and furniture industries and the educational institutions of Cranbrook Academy of Art and University of Michigan. In 1945, the Detroit firm of Smith, Hinchman & Grylls, one of the nation's oldest continuously operating architectural firms, sought to move from traditional architecture to modern architecture, and hired Yamasaki as the new head of design. After several years, he left the firm to found a practice in the Detroit area with two colleagues, Joseph Leinweber and George Hellmuth. The firm of Leinweber, Yamasaki & Hellmuth received several large commissions, including the Lambert-St. Louis Airport Terminal, now viewed as a forerunner of modern airport terminal design. When they opened a second office in St. Louis under the name of Hellmuth, Yamasaki & Leinweber, the demands of travel and two offices and health issues soon led to the end of the partnership. While Leinweber and Yamasaki returned to Detroit, establishing Yamasaki, Leinweber and Associates, Hellmuth remained in Saint Louis and formed Hellmuth, Obata and Kassabaum (now HOK) with Gyo Obata and George Kassabaum.

In 1955, Yamasaki, Leinweber & Associates received a commission to design an office building for the United States Consulate General in Kobe, Japan. The project brought Yamasaki international attention and marked a turning point in his design career, as he shifted from the austerity of the glass box to incorporate modern interpretations of classic detailing. Before the partnership ended in 1959, Yamasaki, Leinweber had designed such notable Detroit buildings as the American Concrete Institute Building, McGregor Memorial Conference Center Building on Wayne State University's campus, and Society of Arts and Crafts Art School Building (now College for Creative Studies), as well as schools in metropolitan Detroit.

In 1959, Yamasaki established the firm of Yamasaki & Associates and subsequently built its office building in Troy (now demolished). The firm's increasing number of commissions extended its reach far beyond Detroit and Michigan. While perhaps most renowned for his design of the World Trade Center in New York, Yamasaki produced significant designs throughout the United States, as well as in India, Japan, and Saudi Arabia. Over his career, Yamasaki won numerous awards and honorary degrees. He was featured on the cover of Time on January 18, 1963. While he died in 1986, his practice remained active until 2009.

SHIRLEY S. OKERSTROM FINE ARTS BUILDING

THE ARCHITECTS COLLABORATIVE, 1972

TRAVERSE CITY.

Northwestern Michigan College was established in Traverse City in 1951 to bring higher education opportunities to the region. First classes were held in borrowed quarters at the Traverse City airport terminal, and the school boasted sixty-five students and six full-time and eleven part-time faculty. Among the full-time faculty members was Walter Beardslee, a young instructor who would later play an instrumental role in the creation of the Fine Arts Building.

The college acquired wooded land on the east side of Traverse City for a permanent campus, with facility construction beginning in the mid-1950s. In the fall of 1966, rising enrollment in the arts programs prompted the building committee to recommend that the college engage an architect for the preliminary study of a fine arts building, supported with $12,500 from the State of Michigan to aid in its planning. A campus master plan, completed by Johnson, Johnson and Roy of Ann Arbor, identified the site for the building.

Earlier that year, Beardslee, by then a professor of history, met Herbert K. Gallagher of The Architects Collaborative (TAC) in Cambridge, Massachusetts, while he was on sabbatical at Harvard University. With Beardslee's recommendation, the building committee first met with TAC's Gallagher and Norman Fletcher in January 1967. Five months later, after interviewing several other architectural firms, the building committee recommended TAC to design the building. The building's final design, produced by Gallagher and his associates in collaboration with the building committee, was approved in 1969.

TAC's design is an open and functional building that complements the abundant pines and oaks on the terrain of the campus. Its series of interconnected volumes are reminiscent of the A-frame vacation homes found in northern Michigan at the time of construction. Two wings form an L-shape plan incorporating nearly nineteen thousand square feet of space comprising classrooms, sound-proof multi-purpose rooms, four small music practice rooms, four art studios, a lecture hall, a ceramics studio and kiln, four offices, and display space. The exterior walls consist of rough sawn cedar and wide expanses of glass. The interior features exposed trusses and the same rough sawn cedar as the exterior. The college trustees selected local construction firm Arnold and Tezak to handle the general contract, mechanical, and electrical work.

The building was formally dedicated on Saturday, June 3, 1972. Herbert Gallagher attended, representing TAC, which donated a tree to the college in recognition of the building. In 2000, the building was named in honor of Shirley S. Okerstrom, former member and chair of the Northwestern Michigan College Board of Trustees and a supporter of the arts.

The Architects Collaborative was founded in December 1945 when Walter Gropius joined with Norman Fletcher, Jean Bodman Fletcher, John Harkness, Sarah Pillsbury Harkness, Robert S. McMillan, Louis McMillen, and Benjamin C. Thompson to establish a firm in Cambridge, Massachusetts. Norman Fletcher and John Harkness had worked in Eliel Saarinen's Michigan office years earlier. As its name indicates, TAC employed a collaborative approach to design projects. Although a lead architect was assigned to each project, partners met to comment and offer criticism. As the firm grew and the number of commissions it received increased, the partners were unable to review all projects, but smaller teams continued to collaborate on designs. The firm incorporated in 1963, and, at its peak, employed some four hundred employees with commissions across the globe. The firm ceased operations and disbanded in April 1995.

Studio space.

Performance auditorium.

ALLAN AND ALENE SMITH LAW LIBRARY ADDITION

GUNNAR BIRKERTS, 1978-81

ANN ARBOR.

The University of Michigan's Allan and Alene Smith Law Library Addition is located within the university's Law Quadrangle, near the southwest corner of the main campus in Ann Arbor. The Law Quadrangle is renowned for its four Collegiate Gothic buildings, completed between 1925 and 1933. Foremost among them is the 1931 William W. Cook Legal Research Library, built with funds provided by the estate of alumnus William Wilson Cook. The library was designed by the New York firm of York & Sawyer, and constructed at a cost of nearly two million dollars. The quadrangle courtyard it frames is a large expanse of grass, ringed by mature deciduous trees.

In the early 1970s, the law school had grown to the point that the library could no longer accommodate faculty, students, researchers, staff, and the expanding collection of legal texts. A faculty building committee was formed to explore possible sites for expanding the library. The committee's investigation revealed three potential sites that would connect the addition to the quadrangle, retain views of the large Gothic window at the east end of the building, and minimize impact on the character of the Collegiate Gothic buildings. In addition, the committee identified aesthetic and functional concerns that the new addition had to address: maintaining the integrity of the quadrangle and existing library building, improving operating efficiencies, increasing faculty office space and proximity to library resources, bringing all faculty offices together, and providing sufficient flexible stack and reading areas to accommodate five hundred thousand additional volumes and hundreds of additional students.

The university commissioned Gunnar Birkerts to design the law school library addition. In the late spring and summer of 1974, Birkerts and members of his staff met with the building committee to gather programmatic information about the proposed facility. Throughout the rest of the year, the architectural team conducted research and studied the existing buildings and available sites. Considering the project many years later, Birkerts recalled that it was clear from the beginning that the problem of compatibility was "quite severe." He then realized that the project offered the opportunity to implement ideas he had developed for underground structures. The primary design challenge for a below-grade structure would be how to illuminate it. Throughout his career Birkerts experimented with and manipulated daylight as an artist would shape glass, steel or wood. In his plan for the library addition, an L-shaped moat or trench wraps around the southeastern corner of the historic library, limestone panels on the trench's inner wall reflect light to reflective glass on the outer wall, where the addition begins, and the glass doubles as a skylight that provides views of the grand Gothic window in the 1931 library and the blue skies above it. Additional daylight is brought inside through a triangular concave skylight at the rear of the addition, at the southeastern corner of the block near the street.

The study and stack spaces are arranged on three levels with a lightness that defies their elevation. The aforementioned limestone panels continue through the intersection of limestone and glass to the bottom floor. Rather than abutting the limestone wall, the floor plates step back from the walls so they appear as balconies, letting daylight flow to the lower floors and providing exterior views on each level. As a result, readers fifty feet below grade enjoy a direct visual connection to the Gothic library.

Construction began in 1978, with completion expected in 1980. Although excavation difficulties brought delays and additional expenses, the library addition opened in 1981. It was immediately recognized by critics and public alike as an excellent and innovative solution. In 1985, building awards juries of the American Institute of Architects and the American Library Association recognized the Allan and Alene Smith Law Library Addition as a "masterstroke of campus planning and design."

Birkerts worked for the architectural firms of Eero Saarinen and Minoru Yamasaki before partnering with Frank Straub in 1959 to open Birkerts and Straub, the predecessor to Gunnar Birkerts and Associates, which he founded in 1963. A highly creative and successful architect, Birkerts was the recipient of fifty-eight major architectural awards and distinctions including American Institute of Architects Fellow in 1970, American Academy of the Institute of Arts and Letters in 1981, and the Order of Three Stars from the Republic of Latvia in 1995. He taught at the University of Michigan from 1959 until 1990. At the time if his death in 2017, he maintained a practice in Wellesley, Massachusetts.

Glass and mirrors bring daylight into the below-grade library.

251

Looking down on the below-grade addition as it intersects the Gothic Revival Library.

SCOTT DEVON HOUSE

DIRK LOHAN, 1992

ADA.

When entrepreneur Scott Devon contemplated building a house, he acquired a site and asked architect Philip Johnson to design a Modern house along the lines of those designed by architect Ludwig Mies van der Rohe, the last director of the Bauhaus and a seminal figure in 20th-century architecture. Johnson demurred, referring Devon to Dirk Lohan, Mies's grandson. Lohan declined to design a Miesian house in favor of designing a Dirk Lohan house. When Lohan and Devon visited the site, they agreed to place the house in the middle of an open area surrounded by dense woods, as if the house had dropped out of the sky. Except for a drive, parking space, and walkway, the stark-white house stands alone, like a piece of sculpture on a manicured open lawn, surrounded by ten acres of mature deciduous and evergreen trees.

The Devon House does evoke Mies's Farnsworth House in its simplicity and expression of structure and space. However, in plan and volume, the house is a perfect forty-two-foot cube enclosing thirty-two hundred square feet on four levels. The staggered exterior elevations, supported by a concrete foundation, reflect the arrangement of the interior spaces. Materials and colors have been kept to a minimum. The exterior is primarily constructed of heavy timbers–painted brilliant white – and glass plates. Glass block and tongue-and-groove, white-painted siding are used for privacy and contrast. Several teak wood decks provide exterior access from interior spaces, and a roof deck provides full views of the changing hues of the surrounding landscape.

The interior of the house revolves around an open-tread stairway that rises from the ground-level entry to the rooftop deck. Private spaces are separated from entertaining and living spaces by their placement on separate floors. Interior materials and colors reflect the colors of the landscape and seasons: floors of marble in some places and hardwood in others, maple cabinets, and marble countertops. Window surrounds of the extensive glazing are painted white, producing a visual effect that allows the surrounds to recede from view, thus enhancing the dramatic views of the wooded landscape.

Scott Devin graduated from Michigan State University in 1984 and joined Coles Bakery, his father's business. (Coles was founded in 1934 by L. Carroll Cole as a neighborhood bakery in Muskegon.) Devon's father, Wesley, bought the bakery in 1972 and came up with the idea of selling frozen garlic bread. Scott took over the business in 1995, added new product lines, and expanded production with products marketed nationally through chain grocery retailers. Devon's entrepreneurial interests led him to other products beyond baked goods, including autos, fashion, and watches.

Dirk Lohan was born in Rathenow, a medium-size town in northeastern Germany some fifty miles west of Berlin. After high school, Lohan left Rathenow to study architecture at the Illinois Institute of Technology (IIT) in Chicago, under Mies's mentorship. After completing his education at IIT, he returned to Germany to continue his architectural studies at the Technische Hochschule München (currently Technische Universität München). Upon graduating in 1962, Lohan returned to Mies's office, where he worked on several significant projects, including the John C. Kluczynski Federal Building, in Chicago, and the Social Service Administration Building at the University of Chicago.

After Mies's death in 1969, Lohan, together with Bruno Conterato and Joseph Fujikawa, fellow associates in Mies's office, renamed the firm Fujikawa Conterato Lohan & Associates, reflecting the changing nature of the practice. Later, the firm was renamed FCL Associates before being reestablished as Lohan Associates in 1986. In 2002, Lohan was joined by Joseph Caprile and James Goettsch, and the firm evolved into Lohan Caprile Goettsch Architects, a firm Lohan left in 2004 to establish Lohan Anderson with Floyd D. Anderson. In 2015, Lohan Anderson joined forces with Wight & Co., a design-build firm, in a cooperative venture where each firm continues to operate separately.

Over the course of his career, Lohan has designed many notable buildings, including McDonald's Corporate Headquarters Campus, in Oak Brook, Illinois (1980), TRW World Headquarters, in Lyndhurst, Ohio (1985), Frito Lay National Headquarters, in Plano, Texas (1985), John G. Shedd Oceanarium, in Chicago (1991), Sinai Temple, in Chicago (1997), Farnsworth House restoration, in Plano, Illinois (1997), Adler Planetarium Sky Pavilion, in Chicago (1998), Soldier Field stadium expansion and renovation, in Chicago (2003), Calamos Headquarters, in Naperville, Illinois (2005), and Seigle House, in Chicago (2008).

Lohan's awards include the Architectural Woodwork Institute Award of Excellence (1980), the Society of Landscape Architects Honor Award (1980), the American Planning Association Excellence in Development Honor Award (1985), the AIA Chicago Professional Excellence Award (1993), the AIA Chicago Distinguished Building (1998), and the Chicago Building Congress Award of Honor (2007). Lohan was elevated to Fellowship in the American Institute of Architects in 1983.

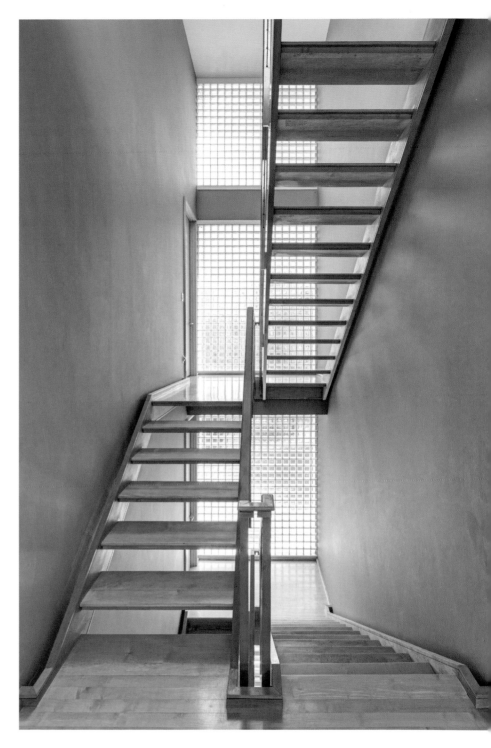

Left, Roof deck.
Right, Open tread stairway
connecting six levels.

CHAMELEON HOUSE

ANDERSON ANDERSON ARCHITECTURE, 2006

NORTHPORT .

Perched on a hill above a rural stretch of scenic M-22 in Northport, the Chameleon House appears to have been dropped into the rolling meadow landscape. The house overlooks acres of cherry orchards with an unobstructed view of Lake Michigan and North Manitou Island in the distance. When Susan and Dan Brondyk decided to build a vacation home, they sought out the San Francisco architectural firm of Anderson Anderson Architecture because of its work in prefabricated dwellings with an industrial character and its unique, finely crafted modern buildings.

The house is a vertical tower rising from the hill to take advantage of spectacular views. Inspired by the austere farm buildings in the area, the house is clad with vertical corrugated sheet metal siding. The scale of the building is masked in a shroud of vertical recycled translucent polyethylene slats hung two feet out from the exterior wall surface on an aluminum frame grid. The aluminum frame grid doubles as window washing scaffolding and emergency exit ladders. The translucent slats set out over the dully reflective corrugated wall cladding gather light and colors from the surroundings, providing an ever-changing, finely shadowed or halo effect on the tower, reflecting sunsets and seasons. Thus, the architects dubbed the house the Chameleon House.

The thirty-two-foot-tall, vertically orientated house encompasses just over sixteen hundred square feet. Built for a family of five, it has a very open, light, and airy feel with shared space and dramatic views. The eight-level interior is built around an industrial-style, open-tread metal staircase with four-and-a-half foot zig-zag runs connecting and offering views from level to level. The main entry at the back of the house is on the third level with two floors below and five above, with the seventh level floating free of the walls. The use of such common materials as concrete floors and unfinished birch plywood walls, combined with such industrial details as the floating metal stairway, exposed connectors, and lighting fixtures, give the house its clean, utilitarian character.

Like a state-of-the-art machine built for efficiency and utility, the house includes many features that could easily escape notice. The steel moment-frame structure, for example, allows for the height and open loft like spaces in the main living areas. The modular design includes walls of structural insulated panels that provide good insulative value and ease of construction with little waste. The concrete floors have radiant heat, while the commercial grade aluminum windows provide light and views. The flat roof doubles as a viewing deck with 360-degree views of the surrounding wooded rolling hills and orchards with Lake Michigan to the west.

Anderson Anderson Architecture was formed as a design-build construction company by brothers Mark and Peter Anderson in 1984. The firm has grown into a respected and award-winning diversified design and construction firm with much of its work in California, Hawaii, the Pacific Northwest, and Asia. The firm is best known for its finely crafted modern homes and innovative use of materials. Each home is uniquely developed for individual sites and clients. The Chameleon House won a 2006 AIA San Francisco Honor Award, a 2006 ACSA Faculty Design Honor Award and a 2005 AIA California East Bay Citation Award.

The current owner has sensitively upgraded the bathrooms and kitchen, and the house remains a visual landmark near the tip of the Leelanau Peninsula.

An aluminum grid suspends translucent vertical slats.

A central, open tread staircase connects eight levels.

275

Roof deck provides view over orchards to Lake Michigan and North Manitou Island.

LINDA
DRESNER
HOUSE

STEVEN SIVAK, 2011

BIRMINGHAM.

When plans were submitted for building permit approvals, the design of the Linda Dresner House's minimalist and brutalist concrete structure created quite a stir among its neighbors in the traditional colonial, ranch, and Tudor Revival style houses of Birmingham. Described by one neighbor at the time as a giant, white ice cube, the Dresner House has become an architectural landmark. Occupying two city lots, the house confronts the street with a stark, yet finely proportioned and detailed windowless façade that belies its open, airy and light-filled interiors. The entrance is a seemingly narrow slit between concrete planes that leads to an entry court open to the sky. The façade, made of specially processed concrete with a highly polished, soft, glossy finish that is punctuated by form ties in a uniform and deliberate pattern, looks unexpectedly luxurious.

Fashion curator and style purveyor Linda Dresner began her career as a model working on runway shows and advertising assignments. With an eye for business as well as fashion, Dresner owned or partnered in several specialized women's clothing stores in the Birmingham area, including Linda Dresner Inc. in downtown. She became well known in the fashion world following the opening of a store on New York's Park Avenue in 1984, where her minimalist aesthetic shaped her approach to high fashion retailing, a trendsetting event that altered the way fashion is sold. Although her New York store closed in 2008, the Birmingham store remains open to serve the fashion minded.

The house's seventy-two hundred-square-foot interior includes two levels with voluminous two-story spaces, overlooking walkways, and strategically spaced windows and skylights to bring in daylight and frame outdoor views. The white walls, granite and white oak floors, and minimalist detailing provide a stunning showplace for an impressive art collection. Thanks to the careful control of natural and electric lighting, both the living areas and private quarters are also surprisingly sensuous in appearance.

For Steven Sivak Architects and Constructors, an Ann Arbor firm founded in 1992, this project represented its first use of poured concrete. Fortunately, Sivak was able to learn from the insight and knowledge of Ms. Dresner's husband, Ed Levy, a part owner of a concrete construction company. To achieve the smooth finish the architect wanted, the project employed computer numeric controlled (CNC) milled phenolic-coated birch plywood formwork and self-consolidating concrete with chemicals that made the concrete pour like water.

Entrance court.

279

View of front façade and main entry.

House opens at the rear and sides.

ELI AND EDYTHE BROAD ART MUSEUM

ZAHA HADID, 2012

EAST LANSING.

The Eli and Edythe Broad Art Museum is a dramatic statement on the northern edge of the Michigan State University campus. It is set at the Collingwood entrance to the campus, across from East Lansing's commercial downtown. According to the architect Zaha Hadid, the design is shaped by a set of walking pathways that traverse and border the site, connecting the vitality of the street life on the northern side of Grand River Avenue with the enduring presence of the historic heart of the university campus on the south. Hadid won the commission through an architectural competition in which the citizens of East Lansing had a voice in selecting the winning concept. Guided by the community's desire to link community and university cultural activity, she interpreted these pathways and movement in the plan of the building, its forms, and the distinctive lines generated by the three-dimensional folding of planes creating arrow-like pleats in multiple directions across the exterior fascia. The use of reflective metal reflects the activity and vibrancy of the street. The building offers a direct contrast to the brick-and-stone university buildings around it.

Eli Broad is an entrepreneur and philanthropist credited with developing two Fortune 500 companies in two industries: KB Homes in home building, and SunAmerica in life insurance and retirement savings. Broad was born in the Bronx borough of New York, but his family moved to Detroit when he was six years old. He attended Detroit public schools and Michigan State University, graduating cum laude with a degree in accounting.

When Broad founded his own accounting firm, he housed it in office space provided by his wife's cousin's husband, Donald Kaufman, in exchange for keeping the books for Kaufman's real estate firm. In 1957, Broad and Kaufman partnered to build two model homes in suburban Detroit. They priced the modest homes so that a monthly mortgage payment would be less than rent for a two-bedroom apartment. With an attractive price and the public's desire to move to the suburbs, they sold seventeen yet-unbuilt houses in just one weekend. Within two years, Kaufman and Broad had built over six hundred homes in the Detroit suburbs. The company moved to Phoenix in 1960, changed its name to KB Homes, and went public in 1961 as the first homebuilder listed on the New York Stock Exchange. Broad stepped down as CEO in 1974. In a separate transaction, he acquired Sun Life Insurance Company in 1971 and transformed it into the retirement savings powerhouse SunAmerica. Selling SunAmerica to American International Group (now AIG) in 1999, he turned his focus to philanthropy.

Eli and Edythe Broad established the Broad Art Foundation and the Eli and Edythe Broad Foundation to advance entrepreneurship in education, science, and the arts. The couple's interest in art began in the mid-1970s, and they proceeded to build an extensive modern art collection. They established the Broad Art Foundation in 1984 to make their collection of artwork accessible to the public through the foundation's loan program. They have also been major and influential patrons of the arts in their hometown of Los Angeles. As longtime supporters of Michigan State University, they provided the lead gift for construction of the Eli and Edythe Broad Art Museum.

Architect Zaha Hadid was an Iraqi-born British architect with commissions across the globe. She was the first woman to receive the Pritzker Architecture Prize (2004), as well as the United Kingdom's most prestigious architectural award, the Sterling Prize (2010 and 2011). She is perhaps best known for her radical and innovative building forms and space development. The fluidity of her designs often defy conventional construction norms and perceptions. Indeed, the Broad Art Museum seems to be in constant movement that can be observed in the changing patterns of light and shadow on its pleated lines. The interior also conveys a sense of movement as perspective is challenged with angled walls and non-parallel planes. Hadid died unexpectedly in 2016, at the height of her creative powers.

*Main stairway connecting
three levels.*

Main entry courtyard.

Main gallery.

Main gallery with second
floor gallery balcony.

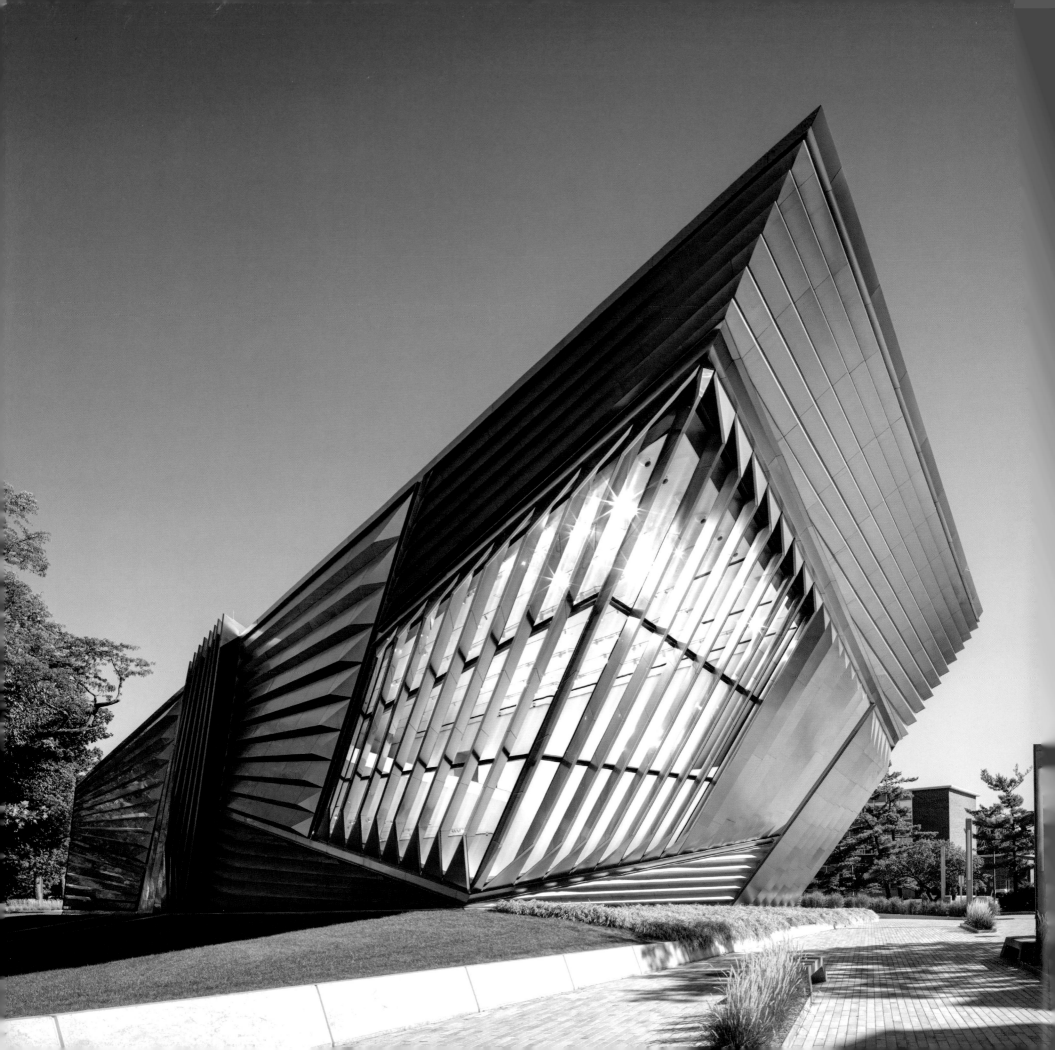

The building reaches out to downtown
East Lansing with the ever-changing light
reflected from the stainless-steel pleats and
louvered window, beckoning the curious
passerby to come inside to investigate.